Karin Bergöö Larsson
and the Emergence
of Swedish Design

Karin Bergöö Larsson and the Emergence of Swedish Design

MARGE THORELL

Foreword by Rhonda Eleish and Edie van Breems

McFarland & Company, Inc., Publishers
Jefferson, North Carolina

Frontispiece: Larsson's so-called Swedish Room typifies her artistic sensibilities. It was created to replace the drawing room with a family room where everyone—children and pets included—could find peace and quiet, as well as familial interaction. Nationalmuseum (Stockholm)/ Wikimedia Sverige.

LIBRARY OF CONGRESS CATALOGUING-IN-PUBLICATION DATA

Names: Thorell, Marge, 1940– author. | Eleish, Rhonda,
    writer of foreword. | Van Breems, Edie Bernhard,
    writer of foreword.
Title: Karin Bergöö Larsson and the emergence of Swedish design /
    Marge Thorell ; foreword by Rhonda Eleish and Edie van Breems.
Description: Jefferson, North Carolina : McFarland & Company, Inc.,
    Publishers, 2019. | Includes bibliographical references and index.
Identifiers: LCCN 2018046304 | ISBN 9781476674063
    (softcover : acid free paper) ∞
Subjects: LCSH: Larsson, Karin. | Designers—Sweden—Biography. |
    Women designers—Sweden—Biography. | Artists' spouses—
    Sweden—Biography. | Design—Sweden—History—19th century. |
    Design—Sweden—History—20th century.
Classification: LCC NK1461.Z9 L368 2018 | DDC 745.4092 [B] —dc23
LC record available at https://lccn.loc.gov/2018046304

BRITISH LIBRARY CATALOGUING DATA ARE AVAILABLE

ISBN (print) 978-1-4766-7406-3
ISBN (ebook) 978-1-4766-3308-4

Front cover: (top) Karin Bergöö Larsson, ca. 1882; (bottom) Carl Larsson,
When the Children Have Gone to Bed, watercolor, 12½" × 17", circa 1890s
(Nationalmuseum, Stockholm, Sweden)

Printed in the United States of America

McFarland & Company, Inc., Publishers
    Box 611, Jefferson, North Carolina 28640
        www.mcfarlandpub.com

For my husband, who understands the importance
of telling the story of this very special and creative woman

Table of Contents

Acknowledgments

I am indebted to the Carl Larsson-Gården, Sundborn, Sweden, for helping with this work about Karin, especially to Chia Jonsson, the director. Now a popular museum, it was once the home of the Larssons. Lilla Hyttnäs, Karin's home, is a repository for all things Karin and her husband, Carl. I am also deeply grateful for the help I received from the association Karin Bergöö Larsson's Friends. This group, formed in 1989, acknowledges Karin and her life's work, for which she had not previously attracted much attention.

I would be remiss if I did not acknowledge Ulrik Jansson, an historian from Hallsberg, Karin's home town, who gave me a wonderful tour of the Bergöö home and provided me with many unpublished documents about Karin and her family as well as the history of Hallsberg. Also, I wish to thank Christina Johansson, Siw Lunander, and Ulla Bitta Pedersen, from the Department for Culture, Hallsberg Municipality for use of their photographs taken by Jonny Pedersen.

I would like to acknowledge the contribution of Christina Högardh-Ilh, whose books on Karin were helpful to me, as well as Lena Rydin, who has written extensively about Karin in Swedish. I am indebted to Ingrid Andersson for her book *Karin Larsson: Konstnär och konstnärshustru* (Karin Larsson: artist and artist's wife), and I am thankful to Carl Larsson and his memoir *Jag* (Me), from which much material was taken. And I must say the same about Alex Freiberg and his book about his mother-in-law, *Karin: En bok om Carl Larsson's hustru* (Karin: A book about Carl Larsson's wife), which provided a great deal of the material in this current work.

I received help from Anne Dubuisson and Dannette Bock, as well as Mary Cate Welsh. And my thanks to Raphael Kadushin and Amber Rose.

I am honored that Rhonda Eleish and Edie van Breems, interior designers of note and authors of several beautiful design books, agreed to write the foreword for this book. And I want to thank them for their enthusiasm for this book and for all things Karin.

I wish to thank my son-in-law Bruce Fleming, an author of great talent and wisdom, who provided me with a model of what one can do, and to Laura Claridge, with whom I once shared a National Endowment for the Humanities grant at the University of Pennsylvania. Her biographies of women are inspirational to me and helped me greatly in writing this book. My stepson, Kaihan Krippendorff, an author, was most helpful to me in discussing books and process.

I am grateful to the McFarland team who were so helpful in pulling together this final version of this book about Karin.

I also want to thank my dear friends who were there for me as I was writing this book: Laura Lane, Amy Singer, and many others, especially Kate Logan. My family has always been supportive of my writing endeavors, which includes my children and grandchildren, and I could not have completed this book without the help and support of my husband, Klaus, and Craig V. Lichtman, to whom I owe much.

Foreword

by Rhonda Eleish and Edie van Breems

We will always remember our first pilgrimage to Sundborn on a spring day, driving up the road passing birch trees and lilacs, to "The House in the Sun." Fresh on the heels of the Victoria and Albert Museum's landmark exhibition lauding Carl and Karin Larsson and opening our own interior decorating studio devoted to Swedish 18th and 19th century antiques, we could not wait to view Lilla Hyttnäs.

Each watercolor of the house was seared like an icon into our memories from growing up with the Carl Larsson books, but nothing prepared us for how fresh, contemporary, and vibrant these rooms still felt or how intensely personal. There was Karin at every turn, her portrait on the sliding doors to the studio workshop, her profile painted on the kitchen window, and the proclamation written on the living room door: *There is a little woman/lived with CL/and if she is not gone/she lives there still very well.*

Her presence and hand boldly announcing themselves in the form of her giant loom and the well-known embroidered tapestries and linens that decorate every room and surface, including the now-famous *Four Elements*, *Sunflower*, and *Rose of Love* designs—each more complex and sophisticated in their deceptive simplicity than the next. Every room was graced by Baroque, Gustavian, Arts and Crafts, Japonisme, and Jugenstil elements mixed together and painted the most fantastic colors, so much more primary and intense than the traditional Swedish painted furniture of the Dalarna region we had come to know from our studies and work as antique dealers.

We realized at that moment how far-reaching Karin's influence was, for in spite of the eclectic layered mix, the rooms of her home are spacious, airy, and have a welcoming ease about them that feels very modern. Karin incorporated into her home elements of style that we use every day in our own design work: mixing styles, modifying furniture to our clients' liking, bringing the outdoors in, rooms that breathe, salvaged antiques, bold colors added to a white palette, natural wood surfaces, letting the light in, graceful lines, modern textiles, and, finally, rag rugs.

These are personalized, functional, and child-friendly rooms. Karin radically broke away from the gloomy, heavy, mass-produced interiors of the high Victorian period in every way. Her friend, the author, critic, and feminist Ellen S. Key, held the Larsson home up as the new, modern ideal for living and raising a healthy family in her influential book *Beauty for All*. Like Key, we admire Karin as a trailblazer who fully embraced the philosophy of William Morris's Arts and Crafts Movement that articulated the notion that good design could lead toward a better life. Karin was instrumental in pointing the way forward toward a more modern, beautiful, and easy way of living that has evolved into what we know today as contemporary Swedish design and life style.

Karin's genius did not emerge from a vacuum.

For a young woman growing up in the 1880s in Scandinavia, she was very fortunate. Her artistic point of view was nurtured by her large and cultured family, the rich folk art traditions of Dalarna, her education at the Arts and Crafts School and the Royal Swedish Academy of Fine Arts in Stockholm and then ultimately expanded and refined among her peers who would become known as the National Romantic generation of Swedish painters in France—Georg Pauli, Nils Kreuger, Karl Nordström, Richard Bergh, Prince Eugen and, not least of all, her own Carl Larsson. This group viewed themselves as messengers in their art for a return to nature and simple, humanistic values within Sweden. They were highly influenced by similar movements in Europe at the time.

Photographs of the period show Karin to be very much a real individual, involved with this exciting time of the fin de siècle. She was active and complex, and not necessarily the remote muse and benevolent mother that Carl always portrayed her as. Our favorite picture of Karin has her peeking out from behind Carl, Anders Zorn, and Albert Engstrom. Rather than being dwarfed by the men, she is the one in the picture who stands out with a playful, confident, and slightly defiant look on her face, holding us and the camera in her thrall.

This is the Karin Bergöö who emerges in her letters, textiles, and furniture designs as well. A bold designer who is intellectually playful, Karin knows the foundations of design well enough to break the rules and create something forward and original. The world is enchanted and follows her lead because her designs are not only refreshing but also made lovingly for her own home and family. We perceive her designs to be pure and, hence, trust Karin and her vision.

Her story is remarkable because, unlike other women of her time, Karin's interior design not only found an audience in her lifetime but has since influenced the interior design of Sweden and the world for over a century. Karin and Carl had a fruitful design synergy, and one artist would not be known as fully without the other. If it were not for Carl's masterful, light, and joy-filled watercolors, the very private art and lifestyle of Karin would not have been widely known outside of their social circles. Carl and Karin's so-called "at home" books took the European world by storm in their own lifetime in such a way that it seems to have surprised even them.

Today, they would be amazed to see that the influence of Lilla Hyttnäs has expanded to become not just a regional Swedish style but a global style as well. Global retail powerhouse IKEA cites Karin Larsson as one of founder Ingvar Kamprad's guiding lights of inspiration, and as the ease of Swedish lifestyle spread globally with the company, so has interest in the origins of the IKEA style.

With the national recessions and political uncertainty marking the beginning of a new century, new generations are looking toward Swedish design as way of life that is attainable, personal, and promotes a sense of well-being. Returning to the farm, handcrafts, entertaining, family, sustainability, good design for everyone—the Larsson blueprint for a happy life is incredibly attractive. So popular is Swedish design in Japan that there was a Year of Scandinavian Design celebrated, and Tokyo Design week was abuzz with the new Scandinavian meets Japanese style design trend called *Japandi*. It is heartwarming to see the Larssons' love of Japanese prints and *katagami* come full circle. Karin has truly touched and influenced the lives of millions.

Had she lived today, Karin would be called not only a mother, artist, and muse, but a trendsetter and lifestyle guru as well. But who has not also wanted to call Karin a friend? We long to know her more and, at last, in this new biography of Karin Bergöö Larsson, we get an opportunity to see some of the inner world of this fascinating woman. Author Marge Thorell has, for the first time in English, brought Karin out of the shadows by exploring in depth her friendships, family, artistic influences, heartaches, and joys. Thanks to Dr. Thorell, the sun rises once again on Lilla Hyttnäs, its happy occupants, and its spirited and ground-breaking maker, Karin Bergöö Larsson.

Childhood friends Rhonda Eleish and Edie van Breems are designers and Scandinavian lifestyle experts whose company, Eleish van Breems, is located in Westport, CT. Their business was started as a fine antiques store with a fresh take on Gustavian formal and country Swedish folk antiques, mixed with the latest accessories from Scandinavia. Today, their design work has taken center stage and their mission is to introduce a clean, elegant, and fresh approach to interiors, with a Scandinavian essence. They are the authors of three best-selling Scandinavian interior design books: *Swedish Interiors* (2006, Gibbs Smith), *Swedish Country Interiors* (2009, Gibbs Smith), and *Reflections on Swedish Interiors* (2013, Gibbs Smith).

Preface

Beautiful and enigmatic, Karin Bergöö Larsson (1859–1928) was a painter, textile artist, mother of eight, muse, model, and understanding wife to a husband who at times could be difficult, but also dynamic and charming. Karin has been portrayed in her husband's famous watercolors in silhouette or turned away from the painter, rendering her somewhat shadowy. Karin was married to Carl Larsson, one of Sweden's most beloved artists. He frequently depicted his wife, his favorite model, in various rooms in their beautiful rural cottage in Sundborn wearing huge hats, hiding her face, or concealing her face behind blooms in the garden. The image is one of serenity that encouraged the "male fantasy of the idealized, undemanding woman, made to be worshipped without giving anything in return."[1]

But Karin was more than just a passive appendage to her husband.

Currently IKEA, the Swedish retail giant, is the standard-bearer for Swedish style, which is seen in Karin's designs as depicted in her cottage in Sundborn. With a lack of fussiness and its ready-to-assemble furniture, IKEA provides consumers all over the world with inexpensive, high-quality home furnishings—everything from whole kitchens to bed linens. With its 387 stores in 48 countries, IKEA, established in 1943, has become popular because it offers a wide selection of relatively easy-on-the-pocketbook, stylish, and modern furniture.[2]

What most don't know is that the IKEA look originated largely thanks to Karin Bergöö Larsson. The founder of IKEA, Ingvar Kamprad, a Swede himself, took inspiration for his designs from Karin.[3] While Karin is known in design circles, the general English-speaking public does not know much about this remarkable woman other than possibly her role as the wife of Carl Larsson.

Karin was once an artist herself who gave up painting at the behest of her husband. Many view her as a paragon of virtue and as the savior of her husband, the one who helped him overcome years of depression, and provided him with a home and family—which he had never had before meeting

This photograph is of one of the two large IKEA stores in Philadelphia. The building is located on a site by the Delaware River in south Philadelphia, which was at one time the heart of the early Swedish colonies. Photograph by Klaus Krippendorff, author's collection.

her. She was also the woman who encouraged him to take to watercolors and create depictions of their home.

But there is another view of her, too.

August Strindberg, Swedish poet and playwright and Carl Larsson's closest friend (until he wasn't), viewed her perhaps more realistically, more three-dimensionally. Strindberg wrote that she was a controlling and frustrated artist, disappointed that her own work had been aborted by her husband's needs and desires.[4]

So what is the truth? Frustrated artist, benign wife and mother, design maven, savior of her husband's psyche and career—or a controlling, demanding harridan?

Born in 1859, Karin grew up in a wealthy family that provided her with an idyllic childhood where she was encouraged to experiment with life. Her parents, Adolf Bergöö and Hilda Sahlqvist, were liberal and progressive. They actively refused to raise Karin and her two siblings by the Victorian standards of the day. As their eldest child, Karin was encouraged to roam the countryside, play in mud puddles, jump over hedges, and engage in arts and crafts, rather than study in a formal educational setting. For the first 13 years of her life, she was homeschooled both by her mother and a governess. During those years, Karin was influenced by her Aunt Elsie Sahlqvist, a hat maker who would eventually own straw hat factories in Sweden, creating bonnets not only for stylish Swedish women but for Parisians as well.[5]

Karin was raised with all the trappings and advantages of wealth because of her successful father, an enlightened entrepreneur whose business was tied to the rise of the railroads. Her well-educated mother regaled Karin and her siblings with tales of fairies and the culture of Sweden.

Eventually, the shy, introspective, yet fun-loving Karin had to leave the Bergöö-Sahlqvist haven for formal education in Stockholm. In 1873, when she was a month short of 14, it was decided to enroll her in the French School where young ladies from affluent families were sent to be educated in French as well as English, Swedish literature, history, and mathematics. Because she did not like the school, Karin lobbied her parents to allow her to transfer to Stockholm's Arts and Crafts School,[6] a popular and prestigious institution. By this time Karin was more interested in crafts and textiles than in learning French. Finally, her parents allowed her to take classes there.

Upon graduation from the Arts and Crafts School, Karin was accepted at Stockholm's prestigious Royal Swedish Academy of Fine Arts in Stockholm. She studied art there and received high honors, awards, and the respect of her teachers and peers. She left the Royal Academy without graduating to travel with her friend, Julia Beck, also an artist, throughout Europe. They finished their travels in Paris where both worked at the famous Académie Colarossi,[7] an art studio that encouraged and even supported female artists, which was not the prevailing culture in art circles at that time.

After several months in Paris, Karin, like many other Scandinavian artists, made her way to Grez-sur-Loing, an artists' colony near Fontainebleau. It was there that her life changed forever—she met Carl Larsson for the second time. The first time was at a ball when Karin was a shy student at the Royal Academy and Carl was a graduate. At that time, sparks were not evident on either side! Nevertheless, once in the artist colony, after a several-months-long whirlwind courtship, the couple obtained permission from her family to become engaged. They married the following year.

Six years older than Karin and a struggling artist at the time they met, Carl came from an entirely different world than Karin did. His family was in a much lower social class. She must have had no conception of what life had been like for Carl. Raised in a dysfunctional family in a Stockholm ghetto, he was exciting, charismatic, and a leader in the group at Grez, and before that at the Royal Academy. But he was a somewhat troubled young man.

While talented, he was often depressed about his lack of success as an artist. He suffered migraines, could be controlling and insecure, and fought with friend and foe alike. Karin would eventually became his solace, partner, muse, mentor, and driving force. While he was busy painting and fighting many battles—some real, most imaginary—Karin made his life work on many levels by providing emotional comfort and financial security—and her family was more than willing to help the young couple monetarily.

Soon after their wedding, Karin stopped painting. This was due in part to Carl's demands and beliefs about women artists. However, according to Karin's namesake and granddaughter, Karin Larsson, she gave up painting after searching her heart. She willingly chose domesticity over the artist's life.[8] In marrying, rather than continuing with her painting, Karin managed ultimately to find other outlets for her genius.

Karin was to become successful in ways she could not imagine.

While quietly raising her many children and prospering in a fulfilling marriage, Karin began her most prolific years as an artist in the small, bucolic village of Sundborn. The National Museum of Women in the Arts in Washington, D.C., considers Karin "the first designer of what would become known as Swedish Modern, who decorated the home made famous by her husband, the painter Carl Larsson."[9]

Now, Karin's home would become her palette. Here, she picked up her art, choosing thread, needle, and weaving over brushes, canvas, and painting. Over the years, her little cottage in Dalarna province expanded to become a true family home, with added-on rooms and outbuildings.

Karin refinished furniture, reupholstered sofas and chairs in colorful fabrics, painted walls bright colors, and made rag rugs for the floors. Her children grew up in this home with freedom, playing and even napping in the formal drawing and dining rooms. They ran in and out of their father's studio and made costumes for holiday and festival plays they put on in their home. Her cottage was in direct contrast to the prevailing style of the early 1900s—somber Victorian furnishings, overstuffed couches and chairs, heavily curtained windows, antimacassars, and rooms where children were verboten.[10]

Karin's textiles—wall hangings, bed coverings, tablecloths, pillow covers—filled the home. Her motifs were inspired by the blue lakes, green pines, yellow and red wildflowers, and the bright summer skies of the province of Dalarna. Karin was enchanted by this area of Sweden, which was bucolic and provincial, and very different from cities she had lived in over the years. (She and Carl found it reminiscent of Grez.) Her cottage created space for her to engage in a special kind of work. Her creations would be imitated by countless others embarking on the design of their own homes—through IKEA.

While her husband traveled Europe, she mostly stayed put with the children. Decorating, designing clothing, and creating gardens containing plants and vegetables common in Swedish peasant gardens, as well as more exotic plants and herbs that she knew from her travels to France, kept her happy and serene.

At one point, Karin encouraged her husband to try painting with watercolors instead of his usual oils, which they had begun to use when they were together in Grez. She wanted him to depict the rooms of their cottage showing not only the children but their many famous guests as well. Carl took her suggestions and soon published these paintings in books. Each successive publication—*Et hem* (*A home*) and *Das haus in der sonne* (*The house in the sun*)—depicted Karin's development as a textile artist, as well as Carl's emerging expertise as a watercolorist.

Karin took her inspiration from England's Arts and Crafts Movement, which emanated not only from William Morris, but John Ruskin and Kate Greenaway, the English writer and children's book illustrator, respectively. This philosophy spread throughout Europe, but was especially taken up by the Swedes, for whom the idea of beauty in the home particularly resonated.[11]

Then Carl died unexpectedly in 1919.

At the time, he was considered Sweden's most famous artist and was celebrated all over Europe. By the time of Karin's death in 1928, the Larssons were all but forgotten. Carl's style of painting was considered irrelevant. His murals were seen as dark and distraught. Those bucolic scenes of his home life no longer moved audiences, and Karin's ingenuity was ignored. Then, the publication of his memoir, which contained information about him that surprised his following, made him somewhat of an outcast after Karin's death.

In 1930, the Stockholm Exhibition, organized by the Swedish Society of Crafts and Design, mounted a show for international audiences with the goal of displaying works of Swedish artists in glass, furniture, fabric, and industrial and interior design.[12] This created a Swedish design awakening, which, while not showcasing the Larssons' work specifically, did highlight some of Karin's ideas: large, undraped windows, clean surfaces, fabrics and textiles inspired by folklore, and spartan décor.

In 1955 the International Specialized Exhibition of Architecture, Industrial Design and Home Furnishing, known as H55, held in a small town outside of Helsingborg, Sweden, cemented the foundations of contemporary Swedish design. One of the delights of this exposition was the everyday sitting room for daily socializing, which brought to mind Karin's drawing room—her so-called Swedish room.[13]

The parlor at Lilla Hyttnäs, depicted many times in Carl's work, was decorated in the traditional blue and white Gustavian style. The room was neither formal nor stuffy but light and airy with plain floors and a raised dais that created a room within a room. Karin set chairs along the walls rather than pushing them into tables. A chess set, checkerboard, and playing cards were left at-the-ready on tables, and knitting projects rested upon a chair. The little sofa by the window showed an ideal place for a snooze. Above all, it was a room for families, not for entertaining or for show. It was comfortable and livable, yet beautiful and well-designed. The lovely textiles with their Japanese influence, the fittings, and the furniture became the prototype for global interior decoration.

We now see this room recreated in fashion magazines and interior design books, using the Gustavian gray and blue striped cover for couches and chairs, or the red checks so beloved by Karin. In both formal and informal settings, the images from Karin's drawing room in Sundborn are recreated time and time again.

Karin's contribution is more lasting than just that of the usual woman behind the man. Karin never exhibited her work, nor had students following her about. She did not seek the limelight. Her aim was to make a home for her husband and children and to use her art in creating a comfortable and beautiful style for living. Her contribution to this style received its due at last in 1997 when the Victoria and Albert Museum orchestrated a show about the couple's home in Sundborn, exhibiting five rooms from it.

Due to this event, Karin and her husband were lauded in Sweden as design innovators.

The author's Swedish heritage is shown in this photograph of her paternal grandparents and family, dated 1922. From left to right: Ruth; Alice; Hanna with Algot Jr. (author's father) on her lap; Algot Sr.; Carl; and Astrid. Author's collection.

Shown here is the homestead of the author's paternal grandmother's family, the Olssens, located in Karlanda Parish, Värmland, not far from where Karin Bergöö was born. The author's great-grandfather lived on this farmstead. Author's collection.

As a woman of Swedish heritage (on my father's side), I was fascinated with Carl Larsson and his beautiful works of art. After traveling to Sweden, I soon became curious about his talented wife, an unsung and somewhat shadowy woman. Because of this, and because I too was a needlewoman, I wanted to read everything about her, but found very little in English. Karin is not as well-known as her husband, even though interior designers, like Rhonda Eleish and Edie van Breems, say that they see her influence recreated time and time again in both formal and informal settings.[14]

To the best of my knowledge, this is the first full-length book about Karin Larsson's life written in English. I am happy to be able to provide images from her work and her life—some of which were illustrated by her husband's lovely watercolors.

It is my hope that people will come to know Karin, her quiet noble personality as well as her work in decorating and textile design, which many say has influenced modern Swedish design.

Karin Bergöö Larsson, shown at her loom in the Larsson cottage at Sundborn. Photograph is used with permission from the Carl Larsson-Gården, Sundborn, Sweden.

1

The Early Years, 1849–1867

It was only a small log cabin in a tiny village, but it would always be home for Karin Bergöö Larsson—no matter that she was born far away and would ultimately live in France and Sweden's capital city, Stockholm, for a good part of her life. Karin's father, Adolf Bergöö, bought the little cottage, Lilla Hyttnäs, in 1875 for his widowed mother, Catharina Björsells, and two sisters, Ulla and Maria.[1] His father, Carl Petter, had recently died and Adolf wanted to make sure his family was provided for. When Karin received it as a gift from her father in 1888, it was little more than a run-down hut from which she would create a masterpiece.

Perched on the banks of the creek that flowed languorously behind the house, the little dwelling had a banal plainness to it that contrasted with the surrounding countryside of verdant fields, shimmering lakes, and deep forests—a landscape profuse with colorful wildflowers, luscious lingonberries, and wild strawberries. With its wooden frame and its ubiquitous red paint—the same rust-colored paint seen all over Sweden whose foundation comes from the famous Falun copper mine—the cottage stuck out like a weed in a beautifully tended garden.

Karin's story, however, does not begin in that cottage. It starts many years before in August 1849, when Karin's father left his home in Sundborn to relocate to a city in the middle of Sweden—Örebro—where he went to work for a cousin. Not long after that he joined a small farm equipment firm headed by Lars Sahlqvist.[2]

This seemingly insignificant job opportunity would have far reaching consequences for Adolf, and ultimately for Karin as well. It was in November 1852 when the large Sahlqvist family, prosperous and thriving, welcomed young energetic Adolf not only into Lars's business but also into his home. Adolf was 24 and Hilda, the eldest child of the Sahlqvist family, was nine years younger.[3]

Eventually Adolf would decide to open his own shop as an ironmonger, supplying ball bearings and other equipment for the railroad industry.[4] By this time, he had fallen in love with Hilda. In the fall of 1855, Lars Sahlqvist wrote to Carl Petter Bergöö indicating that Hilda was betrothed to Adolf.

For her part, Hilda, raised by her mother to be an especially independent woman, lived in Stockholm for a few years during her betrothal. She was a woman interested in the broader world, who found the arts and culture of the nation's capital very attractive. With her black hair, big dark eyes, and dark skin, Hilda, stocky, energetic, and possessed of a strong personality, did what she wanted to do.[5]

And Karin would do the same.

Hilda and Adolf married on November 2, 1858—an event that some thought would never happen given Hilda's propensity toward independence.[6] Their daughter, Karin, was born little more than 11 months after the marriage of her parents, on October 3, 1859.

In a letter dated Sunday, October 2, 1910, when Karin was 51 years old, Hilda wrote, "My beloved daughter, Karin, an equally beautiful and lovely Sunday as this was, Sunday, October 2, 1859…. I went up to [my mother] and said, 'You know, I've got a little pain in the back!'" Hilda experienced pangs all that day. As was the custom, she was put into a buggy and driven around town in the hopes of bringing on contractions, as if the ride would shake the fetus out of the womb. And she told her daughter in that letter that it worked! The following day, she delivered the "sweetest girl in the world and sweet it is the day she is born, Karin child, God bless her."[7]

As was the custom in Sweden, Hilda was attended by a professional midwife.[8] Hilda's mother, called Maja Stina, and her sister, Elizabeth (Elsie), were probably in attendance as well getting things ready and bracing to help with the newborn. It can be assumed that Hilda knew her midwife, who was probably a resident of the town. Because this was Hilda's first pregnancy, Adolf, like many men, might have been worried, even though maternal mortality rates at that time were low.[9]

Karin was lucky to be born into the Sahlqvist-Bergöö family. Her mother was cultured and her father was loving, responsible, and a successful businessman. He had been called a "young elegant dandy," a young gentleman full of energy who was widely considered a man of integrity. In photographs he is portly, with mutton-chop whiskers, carries a cane, and looks squarely at the camera.[10]

For her first year, little dark-haired, stocky Karin lived in close proximity to her mother's family, although she did make trips with her father to Sundborn. In the family home she was surrounded by her maternal grandmother, Maja Stina, and her aunts, Ida and Augusta, and especially Elsie. Her father was busy and not home a great deal, nor was Lars, both of whom were busy at work.

Unfortunately, Karin's toddler years were troublesome.

Although robust and healthy herself, her mother was having health concerns. Following Karin's birth, Hilda suffered several miscarriages before she brought a second child to term—Elsa, who arrived late in 1860 when Karin was barely a year old. Elsa was fragile from birth and did not seem to thrive. The next few years would be difficult ones for the family, even though Adolf was achieving an excellent civic reputation in the town, as well as financial independence. As a local historian wrote, "The life in the apartment at Stortorget [where they lived] was pleasant. But in 1862 there came a time of sorrow."[11]

First, in May, when Karin was only two and a half years old, Hilda lost another child, this time at birth, a boy they named Per. Then early in 1862 Lars became ill with what turned out to be stomach cancer. His wife and daughters were constantly by his side, nursing and nurturing him. He died after months of excruciating pain. At the same time, little Elsa took a turn for the worse with an undisclosed illness. She was clearly not the playmate that Karin had been looking for!

Not much detail surrounds the short life of Karin's little sister or Karin's reaction to it, so it is difficult to know what those days preceding the child's death were like. It can be assumed, however, that these years were difficult ones for the family and for Karin, with the loss of Lars, a mother nursing an ailing child, and a father frequently absent. In photographs from that time, sitting on her mother's lap, Karin scowls as Hilda holds Elsa in her arms. Karin has been described at that time as a small child, dreamy but determined.

On the morning of March 17, 1863, little Elsa succumbed to her illness.[12,13]

The resilient family overcame their sadness. Soon another baby arrived: a brother, Per, born on July 4, 1864. His birth was followed two years later by a baby girl, Stina. By this time Karin was just about seven, and the family was about to make a big move. They were leaving Örebro for a much smaller, more rural town.

Adolf took both business and family to Hallsberg, a town nowhere near as settled as the city they had just left. The family moved to what was called the White House. The structure sat beside a dirty rural route with woods in the background, near the railroad to town. There were few neighbors—barely even a town.[14]

While Karin's family suffered losses and moved forward, Sweden was grieving too for a lost world and lifestyle. Moving rapidly into a period of social liberalization, the national legislature passed a series of liberal reforms[15]—not to the liking of everyone.

The status of women improved, and they were given the opportunity

This photograph is of the first home built by Karin's father in Hallsberg and is used courtesy of Ulrik Jansson from his private collection.

to become teachers, organists, dentists, and hold positions at the telegraph and postal offices. In prior times, before women were given equal inheritance rights, unmarried women could not support themselves and public education only prepared them for marriage. Now educational opportunities were opening for women, and women's organizations, which at one time were formed only to provide charity for the poor, became radicalized. Sweden's feminist movement was first established in 1848.[16]

By 1856 the first railroad opened,[17] and this would be a springboard for Adolf's ambitions. By 1864 the nation had a combined length of 1,143 km of railroad (England had 17,704 km); with urbanization the population in Stockholm, Sweden's capital and major city, mushroomed to 112,000. Gothenburg, the nation's second largest city, became a major port. However, emigration became calamitous, with 17,000 Swedes leaving Europe between 1851 and 1860. Eventually more than a million Swedes would leave their country, primarily for the United States. In 1864 the total population of Sweden was 4.05 million.[18]

Poetry and literature flourished, and women's rights continued to be heralded by the publication of Fredrika Bremer's (1801–1865) novel, *Hertha*, in 1856. This work illuminated women's position in society at the time. Unless widowed or divorced, women were considered incompetent wards of their male relatives prior to the act of legal majority, which gave women sovereignty over their own lives at age 25. Following on the heels of Bremer's work, a seminary for female teachers was established in Stockholm in 1861. These changes in the affairs of Swedish women would be of benefit to Karin in just a few years.[19]

Reading was important in the family, as Hilda thought of herself as a literary person. One of Karin's favorite books was *Lykttandaren* (The lamplighter).[20] She loved to listen to that story in particular as the family settled into their new life. Their new house, while not grand, was more impressive than any other house the family had lived in and was a metaphor for Adolf's stature in the business community. It took about one and a half years to build and contained Adolf's new store, which opened on September 17, 1864, on the ground floor and sold sugar, syrup, hardware, fabrics, barley, rye, oats, butter, cheese, and herring—everything that anyone could wish for.[21]

The house was constructed of white stucco, hence the name, the White House. It had steps leading up to a doorway in the middle of the building for family and friends. (The side door was for shop customers and business associates.) The family lived on the upper two floors. The home was located adjacent to the new train line which ran from Stockholm to Sweden's next largest city, Gothenburg, passing though Hallsberg. The opening of this railway meant that Adolf's iron works would be in a prime position to service the Swedish rail system—his primary business interest.[22]

At the time of the family's arrival, the railroad was beginning to attract new settlers to the somewhat primitive town. It was a humble place, up to that time almost uninhabited, with no school—only a railway station, a restaurant for passengers, and a few houses.

Adolf was in the center of what would become a prosperous tumult with international ramifications. He was closely involved in the cultivation of the town and the surrounding area. He had a hand in developing the Railway Hotel, the bowling alley, restaurants, and other municipal buildings. He also supplied the iron that was used to build and maintain the trains carrying emigrants to America.

Hallsberg's stationmaster, a good friend of Adolf's, was the father of Sven Wingqvist, who, alongside Karin, would become one of Hallsberg's two most famous persons. Sven invented the self-regulating ball bearing. He was one of the founders of Svenska Kullagerfabriken, or as it is known in the United States, SKF—at present a global company represented in

Sven Gustaf Wingqvist (1876–1953) was 17 years younger than Karin, so they did not interact socially as she had left Hallsberg before he was even born. However, Hilda and Adolf were friendly with Sven's parents, S. D. Wingqvist and Anna Lundberg. Courtesy SFK, USA and used with permission.

more than 130 countries.[23] Adolf was also friends with Nils Ericsson, the brother of John Ericsson, the creator of the *USS Monitor*, the first ironclad warship commissioned by the United States Navy during the American Civil War.[24]

Adolf's contribution to and influence on his family was his ability to provide financial stability through his business successes, allowing his wife to create a cultured lifestyle for their three children. The family had an active social life: Hilda hosted dinner parties for officers from the military community in Sannahed in Kumla, the neighboring town. She provided entertainment for Adolf's business colleagues and always made room for relatives. A *Dagens Nyheter* article characterized their home as one that contained music stands in the dining room and plenty of space for parties and pleasant living. Hilda, a wonderful cook by all accounts, loved to entertain. With its musical events and literary evenings, her home was considered a place of "culture, with joy in every room, even in the walls."[25]

By the time Karin was seven years old she and her siblings would travel to her father's home town, Sundborn, so she was able to stay connected to her father's family. Perhaps you could say she had the best of both worlds—summer days with her Bergöö grandmother in the more settled little village of Sundborn, and running wild in the newly developing town of Hallsberg. While still shy and quiet, she had become a little more outgoing and active

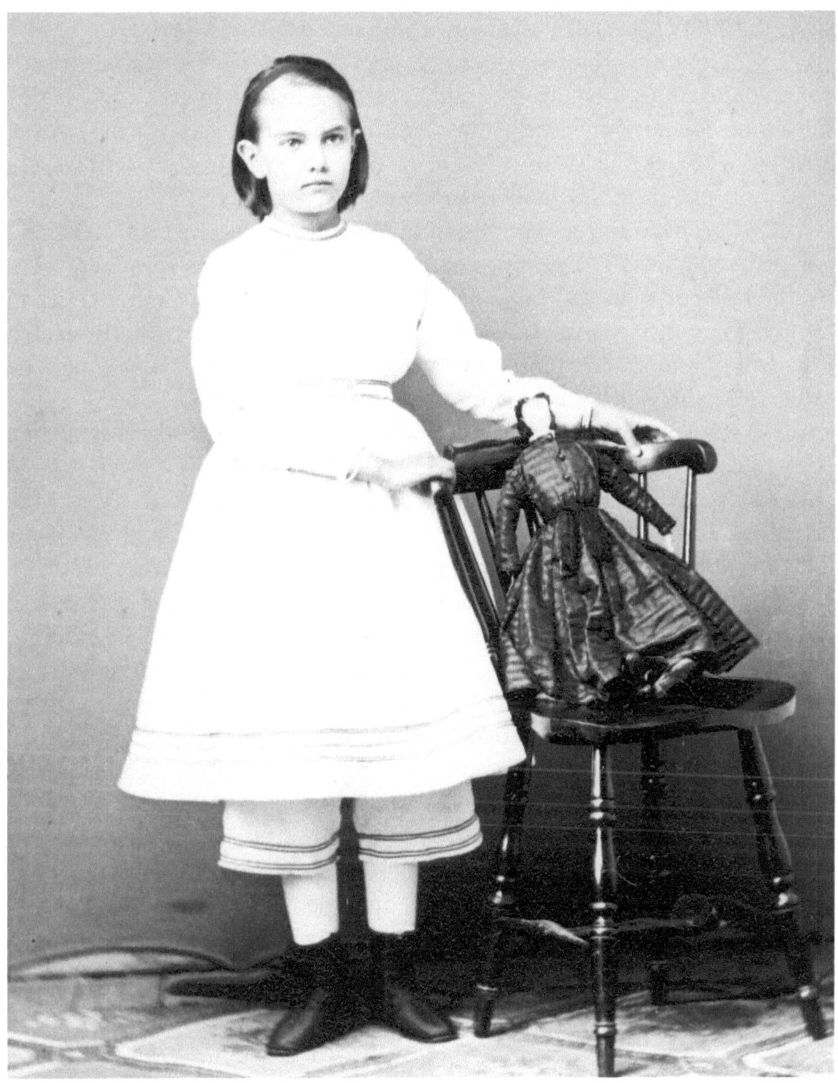

This photograph is of Karin, around the age of seven, in 1866, possibly a studio photograph, posed with a doll. Photograph is from the Carl Larsson-Gården, Sundborn, Sweden, and is used with permission.

in Hallsberg. She enjoyed playing with her brother, Per, and they had many adventures in the little rural outpost.

She and Per, as well as the other children in the area, passed unstructured days free to roam. As to schooling, the town of Hallsberg had made one huge mistake: the town founders, several years before Karin's family moved there, had not made arrangements for a school to be built—an oversight that the community planners could not explain. The nearest school was in the town of Kumla, which was too far away for Hilda and Adolf's young children to travel to on a daily basis. So, happily, Karin and her siblings were educated at home by their mother and later by a governess, Anna Morien, who became a family member. Karin learned to read, write, spell, draw, and sew from her mother and her governess.

One event from Karin's childhood gives a sense of her fun-loving and daring personality. There was a vacant lot across the street from her house that had a wooden pedestrian walkway running alongside of it. In the spring the rough country roads were often very muddy. This apparently tickled Karin's fancy. She waded into the "syrup" and, to make matters worse, she pulled Per and her governess into the mud along with her. Karin could hardly keep from laughing as they walked through the sludge with Anna Morien holding up her own and Karin's skirt. All of their shoes were ruined and, in spite of Anna's efforts, the bottoms of Karin's and Anna's skirts were caked with mud.[26]

There is no word of what her parents said about this adventure!

Hilda, who had grown up in her parents' modest middle-class house in Örebro, was determined to use Adolf's money to benefit her children: first by hiring a live-in governess, and secondly by providing a cultural environment for them. In the spring she took them to the town square to hear German musicians, with their brass instruments and their colorful finery. She took them on walks through the forest, and she introduced them to the world of travel, something she herself loved. Travel would become a big part of Karin's life during her school years and her marriage.

Hilda and her children went not only to Sundborn to visit Adolf's relatives but to Stockholm, where one can imagine they went to museums and engaged in other educational and enlightening activities. She encouraged her children to explore and to make their own choices. As an example, at eight years of age, Karin was allowed to make her own house slippers. She created these little red shoes out of leather and stitched them together with thick, black decorative thread. The shoes were somewhat ornate with buttons in addition to the stitching and were closed with a decorative metal clasp. This was likely one of her first significant artistic endeavors.[27]

At 12, Karin was beginning to struggle academically. Her memory was

This is a photograph of the mural of Adolf and Hilda, created by Karin's future husband, Carl Larsson, and can be seen in the main room of the second home Karin's parents built in Hallsberg. Photograph by Simon Wester, courtesy Municipality of Hallsberg.

not particularly good—she could not remember anything that others told her. She appeared to be afflicted with what we now recognize as dyslexia. While dyslexia is a learning disability, a brain processing issue that hinders a person's ability to read, write, spell, and sometimes speak, it can also lead to behavioral issues such as frustration, depression, and low self-esteem. According to Karin's Swedish biographer, Karin's mother, and later her governess, worried about her ability to learn.[28] But Karin was showing early signs of artistic interest, so her family encouraged creative pursuits in place of scholarly ones.

As she got older, Karin spent more time drawing and accompanying her Aunt Elsie on her various journeys throughout the city. Elsie might have influenced Karin to sew and work with fabric; in addition to those red shoes, she stitched pillows and learned to knit.

These were the first basic examples of Karin's needlework, which, after many years, would lead her to work as a textile artist. But around the age of 13 she put aside her needle and thread and exchanged them for paint and a brush. Not until after her marriage did she again take up this domestic art.

Domestic arts were not as important to Hilda by the time Karin reached the age of 13. Both Hilda and Anna Morien, the governess, were concerned about Karin's education. All those signs that Karin was not learning as she should worried the two. At some point they thought she would outgrow her learning difficulties, but without a proper school to attend and with Anna able to develop only limited skills, both felt formal schooling now would be essential for Karin.

After Karin spent the summer running wild in Sundborn

This photograph was taken when Karin was about 13 years of age prior to her leaving her home to attend school in Stockholm. The image is from the Carl Larsson-Gården, Sundborn, Sweden, and is used with permission.

with Per at Adolf's mother's home, her parents decided that Karin should attend school in central Stockholm. The French School, Hilda hoped, would turn Karin-the-tomboy into a lady of culture—possibly a marriageable lady of culture, although that was not Hilda's main aim.

Karin, however, had other plans.

2

The School Girl, 1868–1877

By the time Karin was nine, Anna Morien was not only governess to Karin and her siblings, Per and Stina, but had become part of the family, more like a younger sister to Hilda. Although both Anna and Hilda had been concerned for a while about Karin's lack of education, they were unclear about what the next steps would be. They knew that Karin needed suitable education, for while she could write beautifully and draw well, she could not spell and had trouble thinking and framing words. Her lack of memory continued to be a problem.[1]

Unconcerned, Karin continued to engage in handcrafts and drawing. While she liked to draw, it was just a hobby or fun activity; it was not yet a burning passion. Karin was happy in Hallsberg—more contented than she had been in Örebro. She liked the freedom of having no formal schooling and of playing with her friends and brother Per and being with her young sister, Stina. She could roam through the streets running up and down the wooden boardwalks that substituted for sidewalks. She loved going in and out of the stores with Anna and Per.[2]

The sadness of her earlier life had been dispelled by this move to Hallsberg.

Karin, while still shy and quiet, liked her life as it was and was unconcerned about the issues of schooling. According to her Swedish biographer, she lived in a "beautiful world of large unbroken plains, ultra-white snow in January, violet colors in March, green shades in summer, and thousands of colors in the autumn."[3] So for the next few years, she was able to be the free spirit. This atmosphere established by her parents was conducive to her creative energy—but nothing else. However, while Karin's education was on Hilda's mind, she also had other worries—specifically about her husband.

Over the years, Adolf had become involved in many businesses and enterprises in the area, as well as in Stockholm. He was a man with many responsibilities and talents, including providing for not only his own family

This undated photograph of Hilda and Adolf was taken in Hallsberg. Karin was probably about 14 when this photograph of her parents was taken. Courtesy Municipality of Hallsberg.

but also for his wife's mother, and helping his sister-in-law get started in her hat business. He also took seriously the responsibilities for his own family back in Sundborn.

He was sensitive and generous, taking on too much in what was a nerve-wracking professional and personal life; his own nervous disposition did not help matters. It was after the birth of their son, Per, in 1864 that Adolf began showing signs of ill health and sought cures at the health spa at Bie. These issues would remain with him for the rest of his life.[4]

Hilda's own life created its stresses and problems. She was now responsible for a large household: three children, her mother, and her sister, Elsie, who lived with them, as well as overseeing maids, a cook, and the governess. She entertained Adolf's associates and loved to travel, so she went between Kumla, Örebro, Hallsberg, and Stockholm whenever she had the chance. She also oversaw a large garden that she would keep up for many years. And if this were not enough, she had those concerns about her daughter, Karin.

It is within this context that Hilda and Adolf decided Karin's fate and future direction.

At first it was thought to send her along with Per to the grammar school in Örebro as they would be attending classes with cousins Richard Stenström and Erik and Wilhelm Wahlman. This suited Hilda's maternal instincts, but Adolf felt that the schools were better in Stockholm, so Anna and Hilda had to change plans.[5]

They decided that Stockholm's French School might be the best choice. The curriculum of the famous school would provide Karin with English courses, high-level math, French (of course), and subjects other than those that used to be taught solely to prepare young girls for marriage.[6]

So Karin made preparations for her new life.

The nearly 14-year-old daughter of Hilda and Adolf was to be sent to Stockholm in September 1873. Shy, naïve Karin boarded the train with her mother at the Örebro station. The train left at 10:21 in the morning and arrived at 6:56 in the evening, thus taking over eight hours to travel from her home to Stockholm.[7]

There were at the time three classes of train travel. The cheapest and least comfortable accommodation cost somewhere in the neighborhood of five and a half Swedish crowns (in today's currency, about 50 cents). In all probability Karin and her mother did not travel cheaply.

Once she arrived in Stockholm, Karin would never really live within the confines of her family home again—but she would always be encircled by the Sahlqvist-Bergöö families and would continue to be strongly influenced by them.

Around the same time, Per was also in school, so poor Anna Morien, "threatened with the possible eerie emptiness of the Hallsberg home, fortunately still had the young Stina to take under her wing and home school."[8]

With the two older children out of the home, the center of Bergöö family life would now move to Stockholm. Her mother rented a flat in Östermalm, one of Stockholm's oldest and most prestigious areas, close to the French School. Her father would use the flat while he was in Stockholm on business. Karin's Aunt Ida, now a widow, lived nearby as well with her three children, Maria and Gustaf, who were around the same age as Karin, and Anna, the third cousin, who was a few years younger. Aunt Elsie would continue to expand and oversee her business in Stockholm and so she, too, was frequently there. Karin, while living independently, was not bereft of family.[9]

The prestigious French School was located in Stockholm's Norrmalm section. Even today that area of the city is considered the center of the capital, but at the time of Karin's arrival, it was dominated by the arrival of the railway in 1866. By then the Old Town had become too crowded, small, and outdated to be the center of the rapidly expanding city—while Norrmalm was light, airy, and filled with trees and plants.[10]

Karin's new environment at the French School, a private institution for young women, had been founded only a decade earlier in 1862 (and continues to this day). It was already the go-to place for the daughters of the Swedish well-to-do. The school originally had been established and administered by Catholic nuns of the Sisters of Saint Joseph order and was located at Döbelnsgata 9.[11] While classes would be taught in Swedish, the young women were expected to converse in French. They would also learn how to be gracious hostesses and become "ladies" in the formal sense of the word.

On that first day in Stockholm, Karin and her mother were met at the train station by a driver from the school. They were bundled up along with their belongings and driven to meet the headmistress, Mademoiselle Grogan. After a brief meeting, Karin was sent to the home of two sisters, Mademoiselles Keventer and Brandberg, who were teachers at the school. She was to live with them for a few months.[12]

Karin did not take to the French School, and she expressed her frustrations to her parents in many letters and in person when she returned at Christmas break. "The second day in school I had my inkwell with me," she wrote of her bad start there, "which I put on a bench in the hall, and I do not know how it happened but the inkwell fell down between the bench and the wall, and half the ink ran out. It was dark in the hall, and I thought no one would see the mark on the wall, but then when we were in English class, Mme. Claire came in and said that we must be careful not to spill any ink because the whole wall in the upper hall had been splattered. I confessed, of course, and she was not at all mad. Still I was mortified, as this happened during those first weeks."[13]

Actually, the real reason Karin disliked the French School was that she had started spending time at the Arts and Crafts School, which was in close proximity to the French School. The more she learned about what those students did, the less she wanted to stay at the French School where she was engaged in learning French and English and history—subjects she had very little interest in.[14]

Karin did enjoy the city. She wrote home in November that "it's snowing and looks so beautiful out; it's like Christmas at home." She was also concerned during this time about her Aunt Ida who was sad about being so recently widowed. Karin told her mother that Ida sat alone while her children were in school. Ida was looking forward to coming to Hallsberg for Christmas, so Hilda wrote back to Karin in poetry, something she did often:

> Aunt Ida wants from us banquet
> Me very glad you can understand
> God give me strength to be the best
> Your delight both large and small.[15]

Around this time Karin made a close friend, Hilma Stenström, who came from Kvistbro parish where her grandfather Lars was born. She was a cousin on Hilda's side and a year older than Karin. Her family lived in Stockholm during the time Karin was living there. (In 1886 Hilma and her sister, Mary, would move to Hallsberg to work for Karin's Aunt Elsie, where they would also live with her until they moved in 1911 to the Municipal House; they lived well into the 1930s.)[16]

Karin and Hilma spent a great deal of time together and liked to cook. In one letter to her mother, Karin wrote that Hilma brought eggs and powdered sugar so they could make eggnog together. Karin was also friendly with Sophie Flack and Julia Carlsson, two young women from school. In one of Karin's letters to her mother, she mentioned that Sophie Flack was knitting "a sort of square shawl of moss yarn with ordinary, though good enough coarse needles."[17]

Despite disliking the French School, Karin was anxious to get back to Stockholm following that first Christmas break, for the capital was an exciting place at the beginning of 1874. In addition to being unhappy with her school, she was not too thrilled about her living situation, either. For one thing, the two French sisters were restrictive—Karin had to check in with them about everything she wanted to do. But regardless of the negatives, the positive was Stockholm itself. There was so much more to do in Stockholm than in Hallsberg. She went to the theatre, which she loved, and visited churches and synagogues and continued to make friends. Her life in Hallsberg had not been social, with the exception of her family, because it was a small, developing rural community. Stockholm, on the other hand, was vibrant and there were so many people—young women—that she could interact with.

During her time at the theatre, Karin met the Draghis, an Italian acting family: father Eugen, mother Inez, and their three children. Once she became acquainted with them, she would frequently attend the theatre with them, and once there she loved to try on their costumes. This costuming would one day become an important activity with her own children who would don costumes and act out pageants and plays at their home in Sundborn. Karin was intrigued by this family since her experiences with them were very different from being with her own family.

On her first visit to Inez Draghi's home, Karin was surprised to be offered wine as a way of welcome. She was also offered something else—an invitation. Inez asked Karin if she would like to move into their house and take on governess duties for the Draghi children. Karin was delighted and accepted—this would get her out of her unhappy living situation.

Later, when she was established in the Draghi orbit as their helper-

Karin, at left, with her dark hair parted in the middle, looks much the "lady" in her long, dark, ruffled dress with lace at neck and wrist, as she poses with friends Sophie Flack and Julia Carlsson (whose positions in the photograph are undetermined). Nationalmuseum (Stockholm)/Wikimedia Sverige.

governess, she was excited to attend their frequent parties consisting of a huge buffet of tea, cheese, sausage, onions, garlic, and many Italian dishes such as lasagna, which Karin wasn't used to but came to love.

She liked attending dance school with the Draghis. She wrote to her mother, "I danced every dance except one mazurka."[18] Karin was living a very social life in Stockholm with her school friends, her family, and the Draghis, who took very good care of her. She began to see herself as more independent, although Eugen thought it was inappropriate for her to come home alone at night—something that she was not going to stop doing, however! Once Karin thought that some activity or idea was the right one, she did not care what anyone else thought about it, even authority figures.

That first winter of living with the Draghis, Karin had much to do in addition to her studies. She managed the daily lives of the family and the education of the Draghi children. Even though Karin herself had trouble with word usage, dyslexia, and studying in general, she seemed able to help the younger Draghi children with their school work. But mostly she did the family laundry, cooked meals, and delivered shoes to the shoemaker, about whom she had a particularly negative impression. She also had this to say about Stockholm: "The worst thing about Stockholm is the sewers."[19]

Karin had many fun evenings with the Draghis: they sang and danced and played games. And Karin loved a joke. On the first of April one year she fixed a friend's watch so that the time was set several hours too early, causing her friend to be awakened prematurely. Another time when she and a few girls were drinking coffee, Karin blew out an egg, then filled it with salt and pepper and set the egg in front of Mr. Draghi—but he discovered the trick right away![20]

Karin was interested in clothes, too, for the first time in her life. It was important to wear the right outfit, and Karin was extremely observant about clothes, noting the special stitching on garments and making comments on the style of garments. She missed having her mother with her, as her mother was always able to make or find something simple but elegant for her daughter to wear.

During her free time, Karin explored Stockholm, visiting with friends and going to the Nationalmuseum; the theaters in town; the church, Klara Kyrka; as well as Sankt Nikolai Kyrka (Catholic Cathedral), or, as it was once called, Storkyrkan (Great Church).

Because the state religion was Lutheranism, people had not actually been allowed to convert to Catholicism until 1873, the year Karin arrived in Stockholm. She also visited the one synagogue in Stockholm. Jews, like Catholics, were only allowed to practice their religion from 1873 onward.[21]

In all kinds of weather, Karin loved walking through the Djurgården, an island in central Stockholm, home to historic buildings and monuments, museums, galleries, and other cultural buildings. In the winter she and her girlfriends would skate on Nybro Bay, the city's huge lake. She made many friends in Stockholm and particularly liked a girl named Anna Narpin. They liked going into the forest together to pick herbs and flowers.[22]

Karin enjoyed the Stockholm winters because there was more snow than in Hallsberg and she could go sledding, riding in a sleigh, and tobogganing with her friends. But she did miss her home and those family members that were still living there: her little sister, Stina, and her grandmother. In one letter she wrote that she "is full of longing to come home to Hallsberg on Christmas break. Today we had a great snowball war in school because it was snowing so fine this morning. It is also cool to go sleighing."[23] In another letter to her mother she wrote, "Little Mother, today we have a full blizzard. It reminds me of my very real childhood memories."[24]

By the second half of the nineteenth century, Stockholm had regained its economic power. New industries, such as the railroad and steel industries, which were making Karin's father wealthy, emerged and the city became a gateway for trade. The population also grew steadily through immigration. By the end of the century, less than 40 percent of the city's population was Swedish-born.[25]

But as much as Karin loved her new surroundings, she depended on those letters from home. In one letter to her family she wrote petulantly, "The fact that I did not get any letters from home, I can not understand. There are so many of you who could write."[26] And she was delighted when she received food packages from home as well, such as the chicken from her Aunt Lisen and those ginger cookies from her grandmother. She wrote that she wanted a "taste of her mother's bread." She also wrote graciously to her father, thanking him for everything and telling him that she would try to stay busy.[27]

Unfortunately, her correspondence with the family was not always lighthearted. Karin went through the motions of studying at the French School and was kept busy learning the diplomatic language of French and the increasingly important English language, which would make her a well-rounded cosmopolitan lady. But she was beginning to spend a great deal of time at the Arts and

Photograph of Karin's signature. Nationalmuseum (Stockholm)/Wikimedia Sverige.

Crafts School, unbeknownst to her parents—not taking classes but "hanging out" with the students.

Because the Arts and Crafts School was in close proximity to the French School, it seems logical that Karin, with her interest in crafts—and her lack of interest in scholarship—might have wandered over to this school. Once there she might have met students and seen the work that they were doing. Perhaps she even sat in on a class of figure drawing. This would have been somewhat daring as she was still shy, but she always knew what she wanted. And by the time she was 16, she had started painting in watercolors and was intrigued by what she saw of the students' work.

For the first time, she realized that she might herself actually become an artist.

As the months wore on, the business of her schooling became a constant topic of her letters. In addition to her "secret" about spending time at the Arts and Crafts School, she also kept from her mother that she had dropped her English course in order to give her more time for sitting in on the classes that she wanted to take at the Arts and Crafts School, such as figure modeling, which she did from 9:00 in the morning until 1:00 in the afternoon on Monday, Thursday, and Friday.

Because she was spending less and less time at the French School, she tried using diplomacy and tact in writing to her parents about switching full time to the Arts and Crafts School. Her mother saw learning English and French as important—Karin saw drawing, painting, and etching as much more so.

There was continuous back-and-forth conversation between Karin and her parents. Everyone weighed in on whether Karin could switch schools. Both Karin's mother and the headmistress at the school did not think leaving the French School was a good idea.

But because of Karin's strong will, she soon convinced her father and mother that she would spend one day at the French School and the rest of the week—even evenings—at the Arts and Crafts School.

In one letter home to her parents, she argued persuasively that the French School cost more than the Arts and Crafts School, and she urged Hilda to please let her go there entirely.

Shortly after these pleas, perhaps because they worried about their daughter being an artist, the Bergöö parents bought a flat in Stockholm at Storgatan 1, one of the finest addresses in the city, so that Hilda and Adolf— and other family members—would have a place to stay when they were visiting Stockholm. Finally, Karin won the argument and left the French School, moving on to the study of handicrafts and art.

The school sat between Klara Kyrka and Hötorget, a city square in the center of Stockholm. The number of students at the school grew rapidly from the early 1850s, and the original building at Lilla Bommen was soon outgrown. In 1869 activities were transferred to a large new building on Storgatan which was designed by the city architect, Victor von Gegerfelt, who was also a teacher at the school.[28]

In 1877 Karin formally entered the school full time where she began studying textiles, decorative arts, sculpture, drawing, and general exposure courses in many arts and crafts areas. Because Karin was working on watercolors, she made the decision that art would be her life direction. After a bit, she saw that perhaps her talents exceeded what her school could do for her. She had begun to think more in terms of painting than crafts, which was the primary curriculum of her current school. She probably knew people who were leaving the school to attend the famous Royal Swedish Academy of Fine Arts. But getting accepted there would take more than just applying. Applicants to the school were accepted based on the talent of their work—not their personality, who they might know, or the finances of their parents.

Could Karin actually be accepted into such a fine art academy? And would she be able to talk her parents into allowing her to go? And would they be willing to pay for it? At 17 Karin knew that, even though the odds were against her acceptance, she had to try.

She also thought about what life would be like at the Royal Academy. She was still living a fairly quiet and sheltered life, still mostly among women. At 17 Karin was girlish, shy, naïve, and uninitiated into the ways of men and women. By all accounts, she did not have interactions with young men, and she did not mention this lack. However, if by chance she did receive acceptance into the famous Academy, she knew that her world would change. She also must have known that if she wanted to be an artist she would eventually have to leave Sweden and spend time in

This photograph was taken around the time that Karin was thinking of entering the Arts Academy. She must have been around 17 or 18 years of age. Nationalmuseum (Stockholm)/Wikimedia Sverige.

Paris. All of this must have frightened Karin and given her pause, but she was determined to enter this world anyway, with all of its risks, perils, uncertainties, and possibilities.

Karin's world did change when she made the decision to attend Stockholm's fine arts school. She would come in contact with other women artists and work with professors of art who were held in high esteem in Sweden. She would move ever so slowly away from the close-knit family that had supported her during her years in Stockholm. And she would begin to travel outside of Stockholm to the greater world of art in Europe.

3

The Emerging Artist,
1877–1881

Karin was not yet 18 years old in 1877 when she was admitted—along with only three other women—to the Royal Swedish Academy of Fine Arts in Stockholm, one of Northern Europe's most prestigious arts schools. She would now begin formal training as a painter. Karin received two small scholarships of 50 and 40 Swedish crowns, which was far less than the thousand-crown scholarships provided for most others in the form of travel grants.[1]

Some of her female colleagues at the Royal Academy included Ellen Jolin (1854–1939), whose works would one day be shown at the Nationalmuseum; Eva Bonnier (1857–1909) of the famous publishing empire, eventually a well-regarded portraitist; Jenny Nyström (1854–1946), who would become a famous illustrator and creator of the Swedish image, *Jultomten*, viewed as Sweden's Santa figure, seen even today on numerous Christmas cards and magazine covers.[2]

Then there was Julia Beck (1853–1835), one of Karin's best friends, a landscape artist of merit. Although Swedish, she lived most of her adult life in France and eventually received the Legion of Honor from the French government.[3]

Another student that followed Karin from the Arts and Crafts School to the Royal Academy was Fanny Ekbom (1862–1940). Known as Fanny Brate after marriage, her watercolor depictions of the rooms in her house would one day inspire and influence Karin and her husband. Brate's painting *A Day of Celebration* (1902) greatly resembles Karin's drawing room.[4]

And one of Karin's dearest friends, Ottilia Adelborg (1855–1936), whose bond to Karin was to be lifelong and whose career was forged at the Royal Academy, became a watercolor artist and pioneer of children's picture books in Sweden. She wrote at one point that she never felt an equal at the Royal Academy ("it was difficult and impossible") and so eventually she struck

35

This portrait, *The Artist Eva Bonnier* (1889), was painted by Richard Bergh. Eva and Richard collaborated on how she should be portrayed: not as an artist but in a bourgeois domestic environment. Nationalmuseum (Stockholm)/Wikimedia Sverige.

out on her own—as Karin almost did. Adelborg settled in Gagnef and today there is a museum named after her.[5,6]

It was during her years at the Royal Academy that Karin would begin serious concentration in the use of watercolors. She was considered a promising artist by her peers and her instructors, and Professor P. D. Holmes told her that she possessed a sure sense of color.[7] This instinct would be useful in the future mentoring of her husband as she encouraged him to move away from the dark oils he preferred to the more lucid and vibrant

Richard Bergh painted this portrait of Julia Beck, one of Karin's close friends, at the Grez artist colony in the 1880s. He has posed Beck with book and Japanese fan, rather than with the tools of her trade—paint and brushes. Nationalmuseum (Stockholm)/Wikimedia Sverige.

watercolors. She would also use this technique again, as well as her sure color sense, when she decorated her cottage in Sundborn and created textiles and tapestries.

Karin and the other women would engage in almost the same training as the men—with some notable exceptions—but would work in two different studio spaces. Studying art was not a practice encouraged for women. Female painters in Sweden, like those in France, studied human anatomy, the history of painting, and life drawing classes. But these women did not have access to nude models so they did not receive full instruction. They were also excluded from state commissions and awards, as well as from participation in official competitions such as the coveted Prix de Rome.

Women artists in France and England did receive training that was influenced by the curricula of the Royal Academies of Art, though their training occurred outside the Academies. They were excluded from the state-sponsored École des Beaux-Arts in France until 1897.[8]

A Day of Celebration by Fanny Brate. Nationalmuseum (Stockholm)/Wikimedia Sverige.

However, during the 1850s, shortly before Karin's birth, the Swedish government was somewhat of a pioneer in sponsoring women's scholarships to study art abroad. Two Swedish women received such scholarships: Sophie Adelsparre (1808–1862) and Amalie Lindegren (1814–1891).[9] The funds were granted for study in Dresden and Munich.

And as early as 1864, a section for women had been established at the Royal Swedish Academy of Fine Arts, with 18 female students in attendance its first year (the enrollment of women was limited to 25).[10] This first group of women took care not to be seen as "bohemians" like their male counterparts. They were studious and did not engage in extracurricular activities as the men did. They felt that it was important to remain decorous. However, by 1870 female and male students enjoyed an easy relationship, studying and attending parties and balls and even traveling together across Europe, spending summers painting under the auspices of the Royal Academy. This was a new experience for Karin—the companionship of men. Up until this time, Karin had been surrounded by female members of her family, young women friends, and cousins, some of whom were male, but younger.

Life would not be easy for Karin or other women trying to enter into any professions in Sweden in the late 1870s, let alone the artist profession. While the Royal Academy, the conservatory, and the medical schools were open to women, and they were able to attend university lectures, public attitudes in Sweden, especially in the provinces, were still narrow and conservative. It is therefore all the more astounding that Karin's mother and father were open to allowing Karin the freedom to decide her own path. Of course, she was a very determined young woman so it is doubtful that her parents could have stopped her in any event.

Karin was happy in this new independent life she had carved out for herself. It offered a pleasing alternative to living a conventional life of a young upper class Swedish woman being presented at court, becoming engaged, learning domestic arts, and living at home with her parents. She was able to live on her own, make her own decisions, and work hard at becoming an artist. She was beginning to connect in a more robust way with the social life of her community than she had before: dancing, parties, travel, and establishing friendships with male and female artists, rather than socializing as the daughter of a wealthy family. This was new and exciting. Still, she had to study and work hard, so all was not just partying and fun. She attended classes and, by all accounts, worked diligently while also attending parties and balls. And she created a number of paintings, few of which survive today. One, a still life, was created at the beginning of her studies in 1877; the other is a portrait of a black man who lived and worked in Hallsberg.

During this time she met Carl Larsson, a struggling and unsuccessful artist who had attended the Royal Academy a few years before her. As he was older than her and no longer a student at the Royal Academy, their few meetings did not result in any further contact. Even if they had, Karin would probably not have been ready to take up a relationship with someone who had the seemingly insurmountable problems that Carl had at the time.

Their first encounter was on a snowy December evening when both Karin and Carl traveled through Stockholm to the home of Johan Jolin, whose daughter, Ellen, was in school with Karin. The Jolins were hosting a dinner and a gala ball. Carl wrote of this event in his biography: "Among others [at the ball], I met there a little Miss Bergöö who, in due time, would become my Karin. But at that ball, I was sitting down with her between two dances and suppressed a yawn as I was making conversation, without feeling a single fiber inside me vibrating. I might have been somewhat curious about her, for a woman I [know] … had just said, 'That little Karin Bergöö is not like everybody else. There may be weeks when she doesn't say one word, but then she'll suddenly open her beak and she always says something that is sound, right, witty, or even funny.'"[11]

He later met her on Jacobsberg Street in Stockholm. She was wearing a riding habit with a high hat and whip—but no horse in sight. Karin was probably not impressed with this rough 24-year-old painter. For one thing, unlike her, he was shabbily dressed and obviously very poor. It would be several years before they would meet again in France.

As pleased as Karin was to be at the Royal Academy, students during her time there—and even before that when Carl attended—expressed widespread dissatisfaction with the school and its curriculum. Many claimed it encouraged archaic teaching based on German art schools. These students of the 1870s and 1880s advocated a complete reorganization, calling for a student revolt. This was in part because of a general turning point in the Swedish art scene against this German influence, primarily moving away from the so-called Dusseldorf School, which encouraged a dark realism.[12]

A group called The Opponents, later called the Swedish Artists' Association, was formed sometime in the 1880s in opposition to the Royal Swedish Academy of Fine Arts, which did not want to have its curriculum challenged. Led by Ernst Josephson (1851–1906), the members of this group wanted modernization; they wanted to be more in line with what was going on in Paris. This battle went on for years. Significantly, Pontus Fürstenberg (1827–1902), a wealthy art patron who would become Carl Larsson's main source of income for a significant length of time (his and Karin's second son would be named after him), was influential in supporting this group of renegade artists.[13,14]

Karin appears to have been involved with this group on the fringes, but her good friend, Julia Beck, seemed to be on the forefront. She was involved in publishing a newspaper called *Palette Scratch*, which contained cartoons (many drawn by Carl), poetry, and commentary about the art scene. Its initial edition detailed the origins of the Swedish Artists' Association. According to Curt Fröberg, who writes a blog on the Friends of Karin Bergöö Larsson website, "The little cheeky crowd consisted of students at the Academy of Fine Arts: Misses Julia Beck, Julia Strömberg, Clara Löfgren, Signe Sohlman, Hildegard Norberg, and Elise Jakobson; and gentlemen Olle Sörling, Hugo Petterson, Theodor Lundberg, Hans Hedlund, Victor Lundberg, and Hugo Hörlin."[15]

About a year after the Association's organization, Carl Larsson was named its secretary and became one of the writers for *Palette Scratch*. While many in the group that Karin was familiar with contributed drawings and texts, Karen's name seems to be cited only in connection with her activities as the Association's typist. Some years later there was a drawing of her by Carl at a masked ball at Grez—*och en bild på henne tecknad av Carl vid en maskerad i Grez*. This was created at the artists' colony outside of Paris after Carl and Karin fell in love, long after she had left the Royal Academy. Carl had this cartoon (as it was called) published in *Palette Scratch*.

Another creator of cartoons for *Palette Scratch* was a student by the name of Leonard Zorn, who would become well-known as Anders Zorn, and was not only a friend to Karin and later her husband, but was also one of Sweden's most famous painters.

The student ferment infiltrating the Royal Academy while Karin was there was driven in part by students from the School of Landscape, led by Edvard Bergh and then later by Per Daniel Holm. During the summer months, they brought their easels from the gloomy attic rooms into the sunlight, painting out in the open, forgoing studio painting in favor of this *plein air* (open air) technique taken from the French method. Their watercolor paintings captured scenes from everyday life and the Swedish countryside. Many of the art students who were studying around the same time as Karin traveled back and forth to Paris and the French countryside and to Barbizon in the Forest of Fontainebleau, the French refuge of the plein air painters. Their paintings were suffused with light, and the scenes changed moment by moment as the light changed. The subjects looked as if they were shimmering because they were dappled with reflections from the sun. These Swedish plein air painters were, of course, inspired by the Impressionists' use of light with color.[16]

Once back in the classroom, following a summer of landscape painting, students insisted on bringing this style with them to the Royal Academy. By 1877, while Karin was at the Royal Academy, these painters formed a "painting colony" on their own initiative that promoted this practice of painting in the open air. The group was led by two of the female students— once again Julia Beck, and her friend Julia Strömberg.

For those Swedish art students who did not go to the French countryside, they initially took landscape courses—not sanctioned by the Royal Academy—that were held in the Rydboholm area in Österåker Municipality, a section of Stockholm County. Around 1877 the courses moved to the historic picturesque village of Mariefred in Södermanland County, which is about 50 kilometers west of Stockholm.

The village was built around the majestic Gripsholm Slott (castle), a fourteenth century fortress situated on Lake Mälaren, which houses the Swedish State's portrait collection, likely an inspiration for the young painters. Mariefred was also the birthplace of Sweden's great sculptor, Carl Milles, born in 1875 around the time that Karin and the other young rising artists were painting there.

The courses were organized by Edvard Perséus (1844–1890), with some funding from the Royal Academy. Perséus was an inspiring teacher, and many of the artists who attended these classes would later form the core of famous Swedish landscape painters, among them Georg Nordensvan, Ernst Lundström, Richard Bergh, Axel Jungstedt, and Johan Tirén, as well as Karin and other female colleagues from the Royal Academy such as Emma Löwstedt, Gerda Wallander, Julia Beck, and Juliet Strömberg.

They advocated for courses such as those taught at Mariefred to be included in the Royal Academy's own landscape courses. In a letter written just after midsummer 1880, Karin indicated that she herself had participated in a Rydboholm course the previous year.

Karin's mother had some concerns about her daughter not only attending the Royal Academy but also sojourning into the countryside with these young artists who were unknown to the Bergöö family.

Karin's mother must have wondered how Karin was faring beyond her limited, mostly female world at the French School and the Arts and Crafts School. Now, all of a sudden, she was traveling around Stockholm and its environs in the company of not only her female artist friends but also male artists who were unknown to her parents as well. While Karin liked going on these artistic sojourns, she also complained in a letter to her mother about how crowded it could get sometimes and how these social activities took up so much time. "Mom, you ask how I thrive here. There are way too many people here, we split ourselves in slight troops and one always has something to remark against the other, there is a constant worry in the air. I long for some time by myself. I have not been able to work with the same force as last year. One consolation is that Professor Holmes has been very happy with us; he realizes that we have not had time to do more."[17]

In the same letter, she told her mother how she worried about the weather and whether she would be able to paint outdoors. She seemed anxious about how much she could get done—having some difficulty managing her time among all the freedom these trips provided. She continued to her mother, "We so often have been away and danced; it was strange here."[18]

It seems as if there were so many activities that the students were obliged to participate in or wanted to participate in that Karin was getting frustrated. There was the Midsummer Eve celebration that was interrupted by a heavy rainstorm during the time the maypole was being erected. There were trips to other areas such as Karlberg, where they traveled for a few days in May to paint outside.

In the summer of 1881, Karin went to paint in Varberg, a charming seaside village on the west coast of Sweden. She wrote a brief note to her father on June 15, 1881: "Now I am happy and well, arriving to Varberg and living with the old woman Hay and her two daughters. My room is very agreeable, close to the city, with access to a small pretty garden and the whole house overgrown with Ivy."[19]

By this time in her life, Karin was traveling all over Sweden. Before going on to Varberg, she was able to attend a big three-day art exhibition opening ceremony in Gothenburg. Her parents apparently did not know that she had even been to Gothenburg and Varberg until she wrote to her father. They were mostly concerned not because of where she was, but because she had not written to let them know where she was. Karin's mother, mostly permissive, liked to know where Karin was. And later Karin, as a mother, would admonish her daughters not for what they were doing or where they were doing it, but because they did not communicate as frequently as she would have liked.

But she was not so independent that she did not ask, or expect, her mother to send her things. "Mom, please do not forget the bed linen and towels…. The best thing I have now almost for every day is my lilac dress, it has probably been bleached and the damage to it, but the navy is so heavy and difficult to wear."[20]

But even still, the world was opening for the normally shy Karin as she continued to assert her independence and to become fully immersed in the life she always wanted for herself, the life of an artist.

Following her years at the Royal Academy, Karin and Julia Beck decided to take a whirlwind tour of Europe's most famous art museums. They traveled to Berlin, Prague, Vienna, Rome, and Milan with the intention of ending up in Paris where they planned to study at the famous Académie Colarossi, a Parisian arts school founded in 1870 by the Italian sculptor Filippo Colarossi. They would be setting up studios and studying art in the wonderful City of Lights.

During this same period, while Karin was spending her days thinking about and experiencing the life of an artist without any financial constraints and with the full support of her family, Carl—a man who would change her life completely—was living a much more complicated life. Karin, however, had no thoughts about Carl, a man whose reputation she knew of but to whom she had no personal connection. And, she was only interested in her work at the time. She was excited to be in Paris.

4

Life in France, 1881–1882

When Karin and her friends, Julia Beck, Hildegard Norberg, Anna Nordgren, and Lydia Wigertsson, had completed their travels through Europe, they entered a Paris art world that was radiant with light, genius, radicalism, and realism. It was April 1881—a beautiful time to be in the resplendent city. Karin was 21 years old.

At about the same time, Édouard Manet had just painted and exhibited *A Bar at the Folies-Bergère* at the Salon de Paris. Oscar-Claude Monet was documenting French country life, taking the same nature scene and painting it over and over again to capture the changing light and the passing seasons. And women were presenting their work in women-only exhibitions, which was one way for them to gain recognition.

The still somewhat naïve Karin Bergöö from the small Swedish town of Hallsberg, whose destiny was seemingly launched when she stitched together that pair of little red shoes, was eager to stake her claim among these Parisian artists. She was still slight of build, with dark hair and brows, and not given to speaking very much, even now after 10 years of basically living on her own in Stockholm and traveling all over Sweden and throughout Europe.

Karin came to Paris at an exciting time for artists—and for women in particular. A month before her arrival, the seventh Impressionism exhibit opened: Monet, Renoir, Pissarro, and Sisley were all represented. Also represented was Mary Cassatt, the American painter, who was a protégé of Degas, and the well-regarded French Impressionist painter Berthe Morisot, who participated in seven of the eight Impressionist exhibitions between 1874 and 1885.[1]

But art was still a man's field. Although wealthy Victorian women were encouraged to engage in artistic endeavors, it was meant more as a hobby or an enhancement of their cultural value—none were expected to become artists who could compete with men. This outsider status was evident at the Salon de Paris.

This is a photograph of the mural of Karin, created by Karin's future husband, Carl Larsson. It is Carl's depiction of what Karin looked like leaving Paris to go to Grez. The mural can be seen in the main room of the second home Karin's parents built in Hallsberg. Photograph by Simon Wester, courtesy of the Municipality of Hallsberg.

Académie Colarossi, also called Académie de la Grande Chaumière, located in the sixth arrondissement, the heart of French academic and artistic life, catered to women. It was established as an alternative to the École des Beaux Arts, a state-supported school, perhaps the most prestigious in the art world, which had for many become too conservative—and which did not allow women to attend. Académie Colarossi not only welcomed female students, it also permitted them to draw from the nude male model—although it charged much higher fees for women than for men.[2]

Among the many well-regarded women artists who attended Académie Colarossi were two women who would become known more for their relationships with famous men than for their own accomplishments: the sculptor Camille Claudel, muse and lover of Rodin, and Jeanne Hébuterne, Modigliani's muse. The British Mina Loy, whose poetry was admired by T. S. Eliot and who was a great friend of Gertrude Stein, would also study there. In addition, two other well-acclaimed Swedish artists were affiliated with Académie Colarossi: Jenny Nyström, the famous illustrator,[3] was a student, and the painter Hanna Pauli was an instructor.[4] The school attracted a number of students from the United States as well.

So Karin was in good company with enterprising women artists who refused to have their art or their voices silenced. (Ironically and unfortunately, they were silenced in a small way much later when Académie Colarossi closed in the 1930s after Colarossi's wife, in retaliation for his alleged philandering, burned down the school, including the archives, so that the early works of such artists as Bergöö, Hanni, Bonnier, and Claudet were lost forever.[5])

Karin and Julia first stayed at a hotel in the center of Paris. Paris was very different from Stockholm, which, while a big Swedish city, did not have the hustle and bustle of France's capital. Karin was frightened of the urban noise.[6] Eva Bonnier was also having a bit of culture shock. Because of her bourgeois upbringing, which was much like Karin's, she found it difficult to reconcile her values with those of the many artists: men and women who were living together without the benefit of marriage or a committed relationship.[7]

Once settled in, however, the young women, who were all sharing expenses—Karin receiving a stipend from her father—found a flat. Perhaps they lived where every other artist lived at that time, in Montmartre. Perched on a hill above Paris, it was remote and inexpensive, as well as picturesque, with its vineyards, windmills, and stunning view of the city below. It was also known for its politics and underground culture, as well as its liberal reputation, which "lured students, writers, musicians, and artists to the area in the early 1880s."[8]

It must have been both an exciting and frightening experience for the somewhat sheltered women from Stockholm. But they managed to pull themselves together enough to obtain instruction from the Académie Colarossi studio. Their studies were interspersed with visits to various museums and walking tours of the Tuileries Gardens. Their visit to the prestigious Salon de Paris was a great experience; they were able to see the most magnificent art there.

In 1882, Karin and her friends continued painting in the city until the heat of the summer drove them to go to the countryside. Julia and Karin had planned to venture out to the French west coast to practice outdoor painting—landscape painting—which would become Julia's forte. Just before they were ready to leave, they received a letter from a friend, Richard Bergh (1858–1919), who would also engage in landscape painting and eventually become the director of the Nationalmuseum in Stockholm.

Richard was well known to both Julia and Karin from the Royal Swedish Academy of Fine Arts. He told them that he was in Grez-sur-Loing, in the French countryside outside Fontainebleau. He suggested that the two could spend the summer there with many other Swedes as Grez, as it was called, had become the special haunt of Scandinavian artists. It would be more congenial for them rather than trekking off to the wilds of the Brittany coast by themselves. In residence at Grez were not only artists, but also writers, musicians, poets, playwrights, and novelists—many from the Nordic countries, but from the United States as well. It was here that these artists were engaged in the new art form—plein air painting. Some five young women—Karin, along with Lydia Wigertsson, Emma Löwstedt, and Hildegard Norberg, as well as Julia—liked the idea, so they set off in July for Grez. They all met at the Gare de Lyon train station for the two-hour journey.

They got off at the small station of Bourron and walked the half hour to Grez. They were greeted by old and new friends: August Strindberg and Robert Louis Stevenson, who wrote that "the village of Grez is recommended for its beauty. There is water, one has told me, with emphasis as if these words, 'There is water.' means very much to a Frenchman!"[9]

The idea of a countryside artist commune was very popular from the late 1890s through the early 1920s, with many European and American artists traveling to France, the Netherlands, and Germany to live in sizeable communities in order to work and study art and literature together. Grez and Barbizon, both in France, were two of the most popular.

At the time of Karin's arrival in Grez, two pensions were available: Hôtel Chevillon and Chez Laurent. Although Chez Laurent was more luxurious, most wanted to stay in Chevillon—not the least because of its hostess, Madame Marguerite Virginie Chevillon. Madame Chevillon loved and catered to her Nordic guests. For five francs, one could have a room and three good meals—with good French wine at dinner even! She would provide a warm bath for those artists who painted outside all day standing in the slush near the river. She also provided medication and support for those who became ill.[10]

So it was that Karin and Julia began their stay at Chevillon.

The village was quaint and full of charm, with an ancient arched bridge, a medieval church, and the ruins of a castle. Its grey stone houses were

This landscape portrait is of Chez Laurent, at Grez, and was painted by Elias Erdtman. Nationalmuseum (Stockholm)/Wikimedia Sverige.

adorned with lush vegetable gardens and fruit trees. The Loing River, which flowed languorously through the village, filled the area with a soft grey mist. It was the perfect place to paint—and to fall in love.[11]

After painting all day in the fresh air, Karin and the other artists would return to the hotel and discuss art over Madame Chevillon's wonderful supper of hearty soup, good French bread, and horse meat in the big sunlit dining room, which was almost like a room in a grand castle, with its long center table and parquet floor. And then after dinner, someone would begin playing a waltz on the piano, inducing a few of the artists to get up and dance. Someone else might sing a song, and the evening would frequently end with everyone dancing over the wide planks of the wooden parlor floor.

It was during these heady evenings that a group of art students, the so-called Opponents, banded together to reform art education at the Royal Academy in Stockholm. They sought to modernize the school by encouraging the teaching of new techniques, ideas, and ideals of the French schools such as plein air painting, paints in tubes rather than mixed up from dry pigment powders, and portable easels with telescopic legs to easily cart outdoors to the riverside or forest. They sought to move away from the dark oils that were so prevalent in the Northern European schools of art at the time. Students were taught from the works of the old Dutch masters but they wanted to become the new masters: proficient in watercolors, taking on the Impressionist's mantle, and moving away from studio painting in favor of outdoor painting.[12]

Karin was influenced by more than just outdoor watercolor painting. The residents wore whatever they wanted to wear. Gone were the Victorian strictures of corset, bustle, and full satin dresses for the women. Instead they wore loosely flowing garments with wide aprons to catch paint spills— gowns that they could wash easily and hang out to dry in the clean, fresh air. Men wore knee breeches and a French beret and some wore wooden shoes, dressing gowns, and a Japanese hat. Some even painted in bathing suits before they went to wash in the river.[13]

This style of clothing, with the freedom it allowed for women in particular, would continue to be part of Karin's wardrobe throughout her life. Some of the ideas for clothing that she would design for herself and her children later in life were influenced by her time at Grez. She would also take from Grez recipes and cooking techniques as well as garden ideas once she began to live permanently in Sundborn. But that was all in the future. Now she was just somewhat astounded by the freedom that she saw in Grez: freedom of ideas, lifestyle, clothing, and food choices. It was truly eye-opening for her.

Karin wrote to her mother on May 2, 1882, "Yesterday we went down

These paintings, completed in oils by Karin during her years in Stockholm and Paris, were provided by Ulrik Jansson from the Bergöö House in Hallsberg, which is now a museum dedicated to Karin Larsson. These images are used with permission from Mr. Jansson.

to the river wall to swim in the moonlight. All was quiet around us. In one of the castle windows on the other side of the river, a light shone. I thought maybe it was some old man who turned on the light in the old uninhabited castle to convince people that it wasn't haunted."[14]

One could be sure that Karin had not swum in the moonlight in Stockholm—or in Hallsberg! Or fantasized about haunted castles.

Karin must have been changed by her experience of being in Grez with so many different types of artists from many different countries. This new way of living, different even than Paris, and this crowd of exciting men and women must surely have edged her away from her shyness. And yet as much as she was feeling fulfilled by her painting and her friendships, it would soon come to pass that a marked change would usher in the beginning of her turn away from a formal artistic career, even though during her school years and at Grez she had created a number of paintings that showed promise.

Carl Larsson came from Paris to Grez at the urging of a friend who was seriously concerned with Carl's mental health. Soon after his arrival, Karin wrote to her mother again, this time on July 7, 1882: "This morning I woke up early, I threw up my windows wide open as I always do. I have sight of the garden and the birds sing so beautifully. From the kitchen there arose an aroma of Swedish coffee. Today, it is a certain Thursday, but it is still not that of a Saint. I made some drawings over at Grez, see what you think of them." She then continued to tell her mother that Carl Larsson and Mr. Karl Nordström "have left the Laurent and come here [to the Chevillon]. They thought that the Chevillon guests had it very nice." She also mentioned to her mother in that letter about Americans from the Laurent who came to her hotel to dance. But it was Carl's arrival that stirred things up.[15]

This arrival of Carl, broken and depressed, yet charismatic, would change the trajectory of Karin's life and art.

5

The Future Husband,
1881–1882

During the time that Karin Bergöö was enjoying the life of an artist in Paris and the spring at Grez, her future husband, Carl Larsson, had come to Paris one last time, a broken man. He was depressed over personal losses and disheartened because of professional failures. And, as always, he mentally dragged his dreams of a real home—one better than the various slum abodes of Stockholm—along with his sad family history with him. Carl wrote about his family: "This is our family tree, such as it is."[1]

Carl was born in Stockholm on May 28, 1853, on, as he described it, "a street which at that time was of ill repute"—in other words, a ghetto. His father, Olof Larsson, was abusive, absent, and alcoholic. His mother, Johanna Caroline Erika Stählberg, was hard-working but bitter. She was forced to support her children because of the profligacy of her husband.[2]

Carl summed up the selfish nature of his father and the burdens of his mother in their early years together:

> In that house, my newlywed parents had used the small savings of my mother to set up a business that was certainly unique for that period—an inn where no alcohol was served. This also turned out to be out of touch with the times. The kind and simple heart of my mother moved her to extend unlimited credit to the numerous young men who generally forgot to pay, and my father bought himself a fine fur coat and moved ostentatiously among the innkeepers of the city, who taught the previously abstinent man how to get drunk.[3]

The Stockholm of Carl Larsson was much different from that of his future wife. Up until the mid-nineteenth century, Stockholm was a decaying urban wasteland with high levels of unemployment, citizens leaving in droves, a population with numerous maladies, and rampant immorality—wars and especially alcohol left women alone, outnumbering men six-to-one. They were forced into situations that led to prostitution and pregnancy. The children who did live in Stockholm were subject to high infant mor-

Painting of Carl's mother. Nationalmuseum (Stockholm)/Wikimedia Sverige.

tality rates as their mothers were largely not in supported relationships and had to enter the work force, leaving their children home alone and open to illness and injury. The average life span was 22 years of age.[4]

This world differed from the Bergöö family's life first in Örebro and later in Hallsberg. And Karin's experience of the capital, living as she did in the most elite sections, certainly differed from the ghetto life of Carl's early years. His family was poor, and living conditions for the poor were terrible. In Carl's case, several families lived in one or two rooms without adequate heating and no windows for sunlight to enter. Carl's various homes were little more than tenements. However, by 1860, several years after Carl's birth, a city plan was produced to promote light, fresh air, and access to nature through a series of parks and plantations. The city government was introducing gas, sewage, and running water. More and more, streets were being paved and the railway brought Stockholm in closer proximity to other capitals of Europe.

When Carl was only a young boy, his father disappeared, but not before he left an indelible and bitter mark on his son. When Olof worked, he was employed as a casual laborer or sailed as a stoker on a ship traveling the waters around Scandinavia. At one point, his father lost the lease to a mill he had bought, only to end up there later as a mere grain carrier, all the while sending nothing home for the support of his family. In those rare instances when Olof was home, he drank, ranted, raved, and consorted with others just like him. Carl wrote that the longer he lived and the more he learned, the more heartless and cruel his father appeared to him. "In an image indelibly engraved in my mind, a man with piercing eyes is sitting there crouched into the narrow space between the window and the dresser and says, maliciously: 'Damned be the day when you were born.'"[5]

Carl's mother, with the help of friends, became a washerwoman, taking in laundry until Carl could help support the family at the tender age of 13. Carl, his mother, and tubercular brother Johan were forced to move frequently as they were evicted from one apartment after another. Finally they settled at Grev Magnigränd No. 7 (later No. 5) in what was then Ladugårdsplan, present-day Östermalm, one of Stockholm's most prestigious areas today—but a dreadful place in Carl's day.[6]

It was a place where evil thrived. There was illness, death, and rotten bodies and souls. Such an environment was the natural breeding ground for cholera and all kinds of ills. Poverty and prostitution reigned and there were bloody fights and murderers and thieves everywhere.

And if the housing and neighborhood were problematic, the neighbors were even worse: "If I say that the people who lived in these houses were swine I am doing those animals an injustice. Misery filth and vice—every kind of vice flourished there—seethed and smoldered cosily; they were corroded and rotten, body and soul."[7]

Carl's lifelong desire was for a home of his own, where there was beauty, peace, and stability. He had tried unsuccessfully to provide that as a boy for his mother and his ill brother. Johan was born when Carl was about four years of age. From the beginning he was sickly. He had what was called hip disease at the time, which was probably tuberculosis. Carl's father inexplicably blamed Johan's condition on Carl, which Carl did not accept, but it pained him nonetheless to think that his father would say such a thing to him. Carl had enough insight to realize that it was his father's own guilt about the plight of Johan.[8]

Carl's mother toiled almost around the clock to care for her two sons before Carl himself was able to help her. Her husband was either absent—blessedly—or drunk. Thankfully Carl's maternal grandmother, Katarina Ekholm, was a solace to the family, helping them whenever she could. She told the boys fairy tales and little stories that she made up herself. These ignited Carl's imagination. Carl wrote lovingly of his grandmother, "From the fact that grandmother had a small pension from the Department of the Keeper of the Privy Purse and Treasurer to the King, one may conclude that my grandfather had done well for himself. On the first day of each month, she and some other old ladies in the same situation had their small allowances doled out at the castle, and since grandmother was then dressed up in her finery, she took the opportunity to visit her married daughter."[9]

And it was this same allowance from the King that helped out Carl's family, without which they probably would not have survived. Katarina's father, Carl's maternal great-grandfather, had been a burgher from Örebro and was known to Carl's future mother-in-law, Hilda Bergöö, who claimed that the Larsson family was a respected one.[10] It is not known why or how Carl's family made their way to Stockholm, but it was here that Carl's grandmother married an artist who was employed at the city's castle, the *Kungliga Slottet*. When her husband died, Carl's grandmother began receiving that small pension.

Carl's grandmother was a woman with a firm belief in the goodness of God. Every Sunday she took her usual place in the Adolf Fredrik Church—the same church where Carl would be married later—and on her dining table she kept a Bible and a book of sermons. Carl wrote that "however capable my grandmother might have been, she still needed God. Without this alliance, she could never have been so wise, so cheerful, so happy."[11] But while his grandmother was a very religious woman, she also loved fashion, dressing as she did in a "cap with piping and an old silk dress with colorful ribbons."[12]

Carl obtained his early education at a school for small children run by a woman out of her home. He then went to a parish school taught by a Mr. Thorman who would again come into Carl's life at a time of deep sorrow. It was at this school that his artistic and leadership talents were recognized. Carl's interest in art came from his mother who, he had been told, had loved art and music when she was young. And of course her father was an artist. So when Carl visited his beloved grandmother, he would look with awe at the paintings that decorated her small flat, paintings her husband had done.

Carl's early artistic endeavors involved scissors. He created silhouettes of family members and friends. He would cut images out of magazines—primarily of glamorous and beautiful women—and then paste them to the wall beside his bed. When he was 13, with the prompting of his teacher, he applied for and was accepted into the preparatory school (*Principskola*) for the Royal Swedish Academy of Fine Arts that his grandfather had attended two generations earlier. In the beginning he felt socially inferior and confused because of his poverty and the fact that he possessed no formal training. Even at this young age, his dreadful family history brought on anger and depression, which he tried hard to control.

However, his natural friendliness and indomitable spirit surfaced.

By 1869 at age 16, he had been promoted to the Antique School, where painters were allowed to study the Great Masters. Soon he was considered an academic and became a central figure in student life there: he was editor of the student newspaper and he began to draw for the humor magazine, *Kasper*, for which he was paid, enabling him to help support his family.

He eventually applied and was formally accepted to the Royal Swedish Academy of Fine Arts. But before entering the Royal Academy, he would use his artistic talents to take care of his family. By the time he was 16, Carl became the family breadwinner—working first as a photo retoucher for *Kasper*, then creating drawings for this same magazine, and eventually illustrating for the weekly newspaper, *Ny Illustrerad Tidning*. He went on assignments for the paper all over Sweden, illustrating what he observed, such as city council meetings, speeches by provincial governors, and railway openings.[13]

Carl was a boy-man who took his responsibilities seriously. It was at this time that brother Johan succumbed to his disease due to a lack of appropriate care. He died at age 14, a shattering event for his older brother, who at 18 was able to save enough money to purchase his brother's gravestone.

Carl was very active at the Royal Academy, which had accepted him based on his drawing ability and his personal interview with its leaders. Soon he became editor of the student paper there. By this time, he was both earning a large annual salary as an illustrator and attending classes at the

Royal Academy. His goal, however, was to make a living from serious painting—not illustration.

He worked diligently in the Life School, which consisted of classes in drawing live models, usually nude. He won his first medal from the Royal Academy for a nude drawing. Then in 1876, he was awarded the Royal Medal, the Royal Academy's finest award, but was disappointed that a travel stipend did not come along with it. He had counted on this as he wanted to practice his craft in Paris. He continued working in Stockholm, supporting both himself and his family. Illustration work was to remain his bread and butter.

It was during this time that Carl became involved with another art student, Wilhelmina Holmgren, who was several years older than him. After some time, they began living together. Wilhelmina made a decent home for Carl, perhaps his first real home. It was a place where he likely found his first comfort. While they were both two poor struggling artists, they understood each other and Carl felt that her support, even more than her homemaking, was what made their home a solace for him. Carl wrote that "without this sacrificing woman I would probably have been destroyed in a certain respect. She maintained my belief in myself."[14]

Carl painted several portraits of her before she died in 1877. In one of the paintings, done in oils, she wears a somber expression on her finely chiseled face, with its arched brow and full mouth. She is wearing a dark almost black gown with a white lace color and red broach at the neck. Her head is adorned with a black feathered headdress. In Carl's painting of Wilhelmina, she is sweet looking and stares directly at the painter, in a way in which Carl would not normally depict his wife Karin when painting her.

Wilhelmina meant more to Carl than anyone else up until that time. He felt that she understood his moods and his anger. They had one child who died shortly after birth. And then in 1877, a second child was born, but Wilhelmina herself died following the birth, throwing Carl into a serious depression. His grief was profound. "The love of this woman was at the same time that of the mother and that of the mistress. She was older than I, and probably she did not expect the relationship to last. She was right, but in a way none of us had expected."[15]

The second child lived, but it soon became clear that she was not healthy, physically or mentally. Carl left the child in the care of his mother and he made his way to Paris. While he was there, the baby died.

Carl, who was devastated by the infant's death and still reeling from the demise of Wilhelmina, was on the point of committing suicide when he arrived in France later in 1877. But he continued painting. His dream

This is a reproduction of a painting by Carl of Wilhelmina. Nationalmuseum (Stockholm)/Wikimedia Sverige.

was to be accepted by the French Academy, the preeminent French council for matters pertaining to French culture, founded by Cardinal Richelieu in 1635.[16]

Several "academies" had sprung up, with the artistic academies organizing official exhibitions called salons. In Carl's time, the Academy of Painting and Sculpture organized official art exhibitions where artists' works were received by the Academy by first submitting a piece of artwork to the jury. Only work by Academy artists (those whose reviewed work passed muster) could be shown in the Salon de Paris, the most prestigious salon.

At a future date, after meeting and marrying Karin, Carl would become an establishment figure in Paris, so much so that when he decided to leave France and return to Sweden—following the birth of his daughter, Suzanne— the art community begged him to stay in France.

But that year, 1877, Carl entered a picture into the Salon de Paris and was rejected, falling afterward into a depressed state. Depression would be a condition that would hound Carl most of his life, but he was often able to cover it up by being overly jocular, the life of the party, and a leader of most of the organizations that he belonged to. He never slowed down enough to take in his depression and fear. And it only showed up in his artwork if observed by an astute art historian or a psychoanalyst. One of his self-portraits, for instance, shows Carl holding a smiling clown—an ironic image in view of the depression and self-doubt which would frequently surface in his drawings of himself. Once involved with Karin—and making her his frequent model—he liked to paint her covered by a veil, hidden by blooms from the garden, or wearing such a large hat that no expression is visible. Perhaps he was using Karin as his substitute to allow his hidden self to be illustrated, but in a subtle way known only to himself.[17]

But despite Carl's depression, his natural buoyancy would assert itself until the next disappointment or failure when he would again be almost completely incapacitated by his malaise. In Paris Carl spent several frustrating years as a hardworking artist without success. He was not eager to establish contact with the French progressive impressionists who were considered on the cutting edge of the art world. Instead, along with other Swedish artists, he cut himself off from this radical movement, preferring to work with dark and somber oils instead of watercolors. This was before the student uprising trends and his work in Grez, where he would be encouraged to move to watercolors by his new friend Karin, and toward the style of painting that the French were engaged in.

Slowly Carl gained some success in the Parisian art world. He exhibited a portrait of a fellow painter, Carl Skånberg, at the Salon de Paris of 1878, but unfortunately the painting was hung so high that few seemed to notice it. When he ran out of money, he was forced to return to Stockholm where he continued to work a number of odd jobs, usually as an illustrator or a cartoonist, while trying to gain a foothold in the art world there. Always an avid reader, Larsson surrounded himself with literary men when he could. It was through a writer friend that he was introduced to August Strindberg. Carl had seen several of Strindberg's plays and, as fate would have it, Strindberg appeared to be living in the same house where Carl's parents had once lived in Stockholm.

One day, much to Carl's surprise, Strindberg knocked on his door. He wanted Carl to illustrate a work he was planning—a cultural history of Sweden.

By this time, both Carl and Strindberg were back in Paris, in the spring of 1881. Their planned collaboration was the beginning of a long-term friendship that would turn sour years later. But in the early years of their relationship, Larsson and Strindberg spent a great deal of time together, drinking wine at Parisian bistros, discussing books late into the night, and enjoying the pleasures offered by Paris. Carl worshiped his brilliant friend.

Strindberg, a prolific novelist and essayist as well as playwright, had earlier engaged Carl in the production of his major creative breakthrough, *Swedish People*, which was first published in booklet form in 1881.

Carl was not without female companionship, either. He lodged in Paris with a young French maid, Gabrielle, who washed his clothes, cooked, modeled for him, and was his mistress. Using Gabrielle as his model, he created a painting for the 1882 Salon de Paris, a painting that was called vapid by critics. The painting, *Chez le Peintre du Roi*, a studio interior in Louis XV style "in which, according to the artist, was to be seen as a half-finished painting of Leda and the Swan, a naked boy and a woman taking off her shift. The picture was refused because of its so-called wanton motif. Carl felt humiliated by this rejection and tore the picture to shreds. He grew ill with undernourishment, overexertion and disappointment. His nerves went to pieces and everything looked hopeless."[18]

Unable to communicate in French and desperately poor, Carl, in his own words, "lived and slaved" in Paris. Gabrielle made another home for him, as Wilhelmina did and Karin would do after their marriage. She encouraged him and provided an outlet for his sexual needs. But yet again, he left Paris for Stockholm, disheartened and accompanied by thoughts of suicide. Then, a short time later, he returned to Paris and Gabrielle. Each time he returned, Gabrielle was there for him. "She was the only woman I needed at that time. Without her, things would have turned out badly."[19]

Carl continued to paint and to submit his work to the Salon de Paris, but only one of his paintings (discussed above) was accepted. Many of his

This portrait of Strindberg was executed in 1885 by the Danish artist Sofie Holten. Nationalmuseum (Stockholm)/Wikimedia Sverige.

Swedish colleagues were accepted year after year, but Carl received only rejection letters.

Not everything was so depressing, however. In addition to his mistress, there was always a group of Scandinavian artists hanging about with Carl in the bistros, cafes, inns, and alleys of Paris. They were painting, socializing, drinking, fornicating, and hoping for their big break—acceptance at the Salon de Paris. There were the usual friends from Sweden and Norway, many of whom went to the Royal Academy with Carl (and Karin), such as Georg Pauli, Nils Kreuger, Karl Nordström, Richard Bergh, Prince Eugen, Anders Zorn, and Bruno Liljefors. These artists, who would establish Sweden as an important art center, were all in Paris at the same time as Carl.

Strangely, Karin and Carl did not meet in Paris. Perhaps each was in their own world, even though they were both members of the Scandinavian artist colony. But then on a warm day in September of 1882 a friend called on Carl and suggested a journey that would change his life forever (as well as the life of shy Karin Bergöö).

On that unseasonably warm day, Karl Nordström climbed the stairs to Carl's dank fifth-floor studio and living quarters in Paris, fearful of what he might find—Carl was still dealing with the rejection of his *Chez le Peintre du Roi* painting. Would his friend be sleeping face down on his cot, too depressed and despondent to work? Would he be roiling at the injustices of the world? Would he be drafting insulting letters to his friends? Or would he be painting, finally?

At that time, Carl was the only Scandinavian male artist to receive a rejection letter from the Salon de Paris that year and this rejection broke him. He had been seriously ill since receiving the letter and was living on bread, cheese, and tart red wine provided by Gabrielle. Nordström had to hold his nose because of the stench of the room and of his friend, who it seemed had not bathed in weeks.

Nordström arrived armed with a grand, seemingly preposterous idea: "You have to get out to the country, out to the birds! Come along to Grez." "You must be crazy," Carl told him. "I have not a bloody sou." Ever the optimist, Nordström told him that he didn't need money. "Something is bound to turn up in a couple of months. Don't worry."[20]

Strangely enough and sick though he was, Carl packed his bag and put on his formal gentlemanly detachable collar fastened by studs in preparation for the train ride to the countryside with his friend Nordström.

And with a carriage awaiting, Carl and his friend headed to Grez-sur-Loing, a village south of Paris. It was here, where old Monsieur and Madame Laurent served him plenty of food and provided him with a soft bed, that Carl felt the first glimmer of hope—he had found yet another home. And

This portrait of Carl's friend, Karl Nordström, overlooking Grez was painted by Christian Krohg. Nationalmuseum (Stockholm)/Wikimedia Sverige.

it was here that he would become reacquainted with Karin Bergöö, whom he had first met years earlier in Stockholm.

While Karin and Carl had spent time in Paris at the same time, there is no documented meeting. Nor was there any reason to believe that she even thought about him during her stay there. While this relationship that would flower in Grez was one that apparently enhanced both of their lives, it must be said that it seemed almost preposterous that the shy Karin would be attracted to this bear of a man with a somewhat sordid past, no money, limited professional prospects, and a decidedly strange personality. If one were to ask with whom Karin Bergöö would finally have a relationship—or even marry—no one in their right mind would have responded, "But of course, Carl Larsson!" Even more strange than that, why in the world would her parents ever consent to such an arrangement? No! They would not. They could not.

6

The Courtship, 1882

Carl Larsson, with all his faults, was always very popular no matter where he went. He was gay, pugnacious, independent, yet gentle of mind. He was tall, well-built, with a reddish face. He liked to wear rakish clothing such as a long, yellow-brown smoking jacket. He no doubt exuded sexuality and had the demeanor of a man who has known many women. While he could be terribly insecure, it did not usually show in his behaviors. He had a booming voice so everyone always knew where he could be found—usually in a place where there was fun and great conversation.[1]

One can imagine the fuss that was made of him when he arrived at the Chevillon, for he was well known to the Scandinavian artists in Grez. He expressed his pleasure at the calm and peace of the place and the streaks of sunlight that poured into the window of his room, but he was still depressed. He wrote in his memoir: "The nights—it was like a hard arm had gripped my bowels and wrung them around. But anyhow—daytime I held myself upwards, I ate, and I took a swim in the river. It was then that I got watercolors and paper in my hand and I painted my first aquarelle, *Forbidden Fruit*. I saw it wasn't very good—but in Stockholm they wanted the watercolor paintings."[2]

He immediately entered the social scene in Grez. His troubled spirits were soon lifted with the reappearance of the young woman from the Royal Academy. "Then came the most important turning point—now Karin came! Dreaming, with her large, round cow's eyes, with her little potato nose in the middle of the face, where noses usually are, but here, it had a very special effect."[3]

During that spring and summer of 1882, Carl and Karin spent a great deal of time together. While less naïve than she had been when living in Stockholm—and less shy—she was still no match for the dominant, domineering Carl, who was sick and poor besides. However, he had that commanding presence, he was not totally unknown to her, and he was a leader of not only that group in Grez, but also previously at the Royal

65

Academy in Stockholm. To say he was charismatic was an understatement.

Karin, with little experience of men, was bowled over by his attention, his friendliness, his obvious talent, and perhaps by his insecurities. They ate and painted together, discussed art, and took long walks. She, whose use of color was always exquisite and who was using watercolors while he was still using oils, found that Carl took her advice on things—like thinking about switching to watercolor paints. This might have been exciting for her—to be even a little bit of a mentor to this big bear of a man. Carl Larsson wrote in detail in his memoirs of his artistic breakthrough using watercolors. "It [this first watercolor] was thin and dry, but I nevertheless sent it to Stockholm, where people started fighting about it. I had called it *The Forbidden Fruit*, and it showed an old farm woman who had come upon a little girl filling her apron with cherries."[4]

What he does not write about in the memoir is that it was Karin who influenced this breakthrough, nor did he mention how she influenced so much of his art that followed, which led to his fame as a great watercolorist. That was left for others to recognize. But Karin did not seem to mind that her mentorship of Carl went unacknowledged by him—or at least if she did, she never wrote about it. What she did write about was her happiness.

Thus, while working together throughout the spring, they fell in love.

It was not long before their friends realized it—perhaps before they did—that Carl and Karin were a couple. By the time August came, they probably understood, too, that something was going on between them, but nothing was said about their feelings for each other for some time. Then one clear day in September, Carl and Karin went to the nearby village of Montcourt to eat grapes, pausing on their way home by the bridge in Grez for a first kiss. As Karin wrote to her parents on September 13, 1882, "I have never seen my life so clearly in front of me now and there is not the slightest trace of doubt; I have never met a person who has given me such support as he."[5]

While Carl wrote in his memoir, "Karin put her arm in mine, her little finger brushed against my hand, and I burst out: How I love you!"[6]

Carl wrote to Karin's parents: "Herr and Fru Bergöö, I love your daughter. A few superlatives to express the extent of my love are but unnecessary, when I say that I love her as an honest man should love an honest girl."[7]

Adolf wrote back to Carl: "You write: 'What am I? Not much yet.' You suffice for us provided you are a Man in the full sense of the word."[8]

Surprisingly, Carl did not know that his intended was a woman from a wealthy family. On a bus during one of his trips back to Paris in September, one of his friends, Theodor Lundberg, told Carl that Karin's father was a successful businessman. Prior to this time, Carl thought that she was "pitiable and poor" like everyone else in Grez. Most of Carl's friends had little money; they would help each other out—whoever had money gave to those who did not. Carl thought this was the case with Karin—that her friends had contributed the means for her to stay in Grez.[9]

As to these wealthy parents, we may wonder what they thought of their daughter's choice of a husband who described himself as "ugly, with a washed-out complexion, my face full of pimples. I was already going bald. And add to that, back in Sweden I had poor parents who I had long supported and who would soon be totally dependent on me."[10]

Once again, Karin's parents would make a decision that was not in keeping with the mores of their society. They agreed to the marriage of their daughter, even though the husband-to-be was a man without money and seemingly without prospects. "We trust Karin's judgment. We believe that she can only love an honest man," they said.[11]

This was definitely not something that was done in Hallsberg—or in Swedish society, for that matter. To allow a daughter, or even a son, to marry someone so far down the social ladder was not typical, certainly not by upper-middle class parents in any case. Yes, he was regarded as a very fine cartoonist and illustrator, from which he earned his living, but he was willing to give that all up to become an artist, a real artist, without any real recognition from the Paris art community. However, Karin's father, whose family was comprised of shopkeepers, and her mother, who came from a family of millers and millwrights, had the greatest of confidence in their children.

Karin, determined and strong-willed, had made incredible choices as a girl and young

This photograph of Carl was taken in 1888 when Karin was about 29 years old and the couple had been married for several years. Nationalmuseum (Stockholm)/Wikimedia Sverige.

woman, choices that would allow her to pursue, enthusiastically and with total conviction, her art. She argued over the years with her parents about allowing her to follow her passion. She must have been scared living in the capital of Sweden mostly by herself. She also must have felt concerned about her abilities and how she would interact with other artists, especially men. Nonetheless she made many decisions and overcame many problems in order to pursue her profession all the way to the Académie Colarossi. Was it a lark? Did she do this because she had nothing better to do? Did she travel to Paris simply because she had the money to do so? Had she become bored of practicing her art?

If she chose art against all odds as a young girl, why then did she give it all up to become the wife of a demanding, neurotic, egocentric, and to some degree severely damaged man—a man who basically demanded that she give up her own professional life to serve his? And give it up she must, if she was to continue in this relationship, as Carl did not support the idea of female artists. But that decision was yet to come.

7

The Engagement, 1882–1883

The year Karin and Carl reconnected would mark great changes for Karin. Carl, too, would find his life in a different place than before his arrival at Grez. His betrothal to Karin improved his social standing, and his future as a recognized artist was beginning to unfold, too. He would soon be hailed as the master at this plein air medium. Carl's watercolors held a certain luminosity; they seemed to be painted almost effortlessly. Carl wrote: "I looked at Nature for the first time. I chucked the bizarre into the trash heap and dumped my remarkable combination of ideas into the lake. They can stay there. I have not given Nature a wide embrace, no matter how simple it may be."[1]

During that summer of 1882, the couple spent countless hours together painting, picnicking, dancing, dining, drinking, swimming, and talking about their art while they were engaged and still living in Grez. Carl, however, believed he could not and should not lure "a young girl child along a rocky road."[2] Yet his love for Karin and his resolve to make a good life for her was evident in one of the letters he wrote to her parents. "Shall I get it over with quickly? I love your daughter! Superlatives that would indicate the degree of my love are unnecessary, for I am saying I love her as a man of honor should love a young woman of honor. Who am I? There is not much to show yet! It is not my present position that confirms me in the hope of proving worthy of your daughter, but my firm belief and conviction in the future that I can create with my strength and willpower. My love has raised me from the depths of despondency; but I need a year of assiduous endeavor to now build and plan the future."[3]

Meanwhile Carl was still under the weather with stomach pains and daytime shivers but, as always, he was able to paint and claimed he "felt like Atlas."[4] This would be a continuing story with Karin's husband: he would never admit to frailties unless he was absolutely driven to it, and then he would tell Karin and expect her to fix things. Almost from the beginning, he found himself leaning on her for emotional support and for artistic direction.[5]

It has been suggested that Karin told Carl not only to work outside with watercolors but also that he should consider using subjects that were more quotidian. So his paintings, completed outdoors, were landscapes, but these paintings possessed a more immediate view than a panoramic one, usually with a lone figure in the foreground. Together they began to examine the work of Jules Bastien-Lepage (1848–1884), the French painter closely associated with naturalism, and they particularly liked Bastien-Lepage's watercolor painting, *The Hayfield* (1875), which captured a rural subject that was reminiscent of places from Carl's childhood.[6]

According to Görel Cavalli-Björkman, this change in perspective, perhaps brought on by his association with Karin, began Larsson's first period of greatness. He began painting more simplistically. He had been advised by his teacher at the Royal Academy, Fredrik Wilhelm Scholander, "to stop training for the remarkable, the striking, the never before done, but rather leave such things to those who had lost their heads."[7]

This advice from his mentor mirrored what Karin was saying also—simplify. Under his soon-to-be-wife's tutelage and guidance during the summer and fall of their renewed acquaintance and ensuing betrothal, Carl did finally heed the advice of his teacher—and Karin.

At this point, Karin was still painting as well and engaged in experimental art, too. One of her most notable works from this time period featured Mère Morot, who was one of the more colorful elderly peasant women in Grez. In Karin's painting of Mère Morot, Karin exhibited a technique more stylistically similar to *The Hayfield* than Carl's would be in the various paintings he created in Grez, in which he also used Mère Morot as the subject.

In Karin's version, the woman is standing in the center of the picture in a field muted by the painter's intuitive use of watercolors. It is a beautiful rendering, first in a sketch and later in watercolor, with subtle colors and an indistinct background. Here, the lone figure of Mère Morot provides depth to the painting, with the woman facing away from the artist so there is a feeling of solitude and contentment. There has been very little critical discussion about Karin's 37 × 26 cm. (14.6 × 10.2 in.) watercolor painted in Grez, but the motif, a woman standing in a garden, shows up in numerous places in Carl's oeuvre.

During that same time, the summer and fall of 1882, Carl captured the same scene on his canvas and called it *Pumpkins,* changing the name several times (first to *Mère Morot* and then to *Autumn*). Carl's painting, submitted to the Salon de Paris in the spring of 1883, won a third-place medal. Meanwhile, Karin started to become interested in and influenced by Japanese art, which will be seen later in her tapestries and needlework—and in Carl's art.

This watercolor of Mère Morot, which Karin completed while at Grez, inspired Carl to use watercolors. Nationalmuseum (Stockholm)/Wikimedia Sverige.

This is Carl's portrait of Mère Morot, which was painted after Karin's. The similarities are evident. Nationalmuseum (Stockholm)/Wikimedia Sverige.

Toward the end of October 1882, Carl left Grez to return to Paris, where he had some unfinished business to take care of. He had left behind his mistress and model, the young and adoring Gabrielle, when he traveled to Grez. When he told her that their relationship was over and that he was going to marry, she was desolate and inconsolable. She had a great love for Carl, and, while he was fond of her and grateful to her, he knew the time had come for him to give up his various lovers—there were others beside Gabrielle—and create a more stable partnership with Karin.[8]

Fall came and went. Carl returned to Grez. Karin returned to Paris, along with Julia Beck and Eva Bonnier, to their studio where she would study under Alfred Stevens (1823–1906), a Belgian. He was a well-regarded artist and teacher, known for his paintings of beautiful women. It is quite notable that he was willing to take on the young Karin Bergöö as a student.

Karin's father, Adolf, was more than willing to continue to pay for her further education, even though she was soon to be married. But Carl had been anxious about Karin's success at the Colarossi atelier, where she was viewed as a very promising artist. In a letter to his mother-in-law, Carl wrote "to my horror, I have been told that she is very successful."[9]

Karin's continuing involvement in painting apparently came to an end when she wrote home saying that Carl would not like her to continue working as an artist. She had had an argument with Julia Beck just before writing the letter to her mother. Their discussion was about Karin giving up painting for marriage. She and Julia's relationship became strained over Karin's abdication of her life as an artist. This caused Karin to refuse to discuss painting with Julia, either continuing with it or giving it up. And for her part, Julia never did marry but was able to produce art successfully, winning awards and recognition in France—although she did have a relationship with a journalist who used the pen name Spada.[10] Once married and back in Grez with Carl, all Karin did was stand in the kitchen and cook.

Quite a change for a woman who was so determined to make art "her life's work."

It seems clear from letters and discussions with her family that Karin did not complain about being forced to give up painting, but it did seem that Carl's insistence that she be the "wife of an artist" rather than an artist herself might have looked like coercion. Her granddaughter—and namesake—Karin Larsson asserts that she had no regrets about giving up art for Carl.[11,12]

And it must be remembered that Karin was possessed of a very strong personality. It is difficult to imagine her giving up something she truly wanted without a fight. What is unclear is the why. Why did she so readily put down her brushes and easel? Over the years, letters and testimony from friends claimed that Karin could certainly hold her own against Carl. Perhaps the answer is that she wanted love and family more than fame and art, especially given that art as a profession for a woman was difficult—if not almost impossible.

In these times, at the end of the nineteenth century and even into the twentieth in Sweden and in France, women could be wives and mothers or artists. And certainly two artists married or living together would not work. With very few exceptions, women could not, in artistic circles, be both wife and artist.

Hanna and Georg Pauli were the rare couple who did manage to do this, as both were painters; however, Hanna's output after marriage was limited. Hildegard Thorell, a very distant relative of mine, was able to be an artist and a wife, but her husband was an accountant so there was no hint of competition. Eva Bonnier, wealthy and well-regarded as an artist, certainly could not have both. She, too, was very critical of Karin for giving up art for marriage, especially marriage to Carl, as we shall see later on from some of her letters to her own family.

Karin must have been upset about the criticism she was receiving from her closest friends, Julia and especially from Eva Bonnier, and mentioned this in a letter to her mother. She told Hilda that they were not happy about her choice, but Karin was never one to care what other people thought—not after moving to Stockholm at age 13, leaving the French School, becoming an artist, and moving to Paris. And she didn't care now what people were saying about her choice to give up art and marry Carl Larsson. She had a singular vision. Once it had been art. Now it was Carl and creating a family. For Karin, her own path was all that mattered.[13]

And Carl had been very dynamic in wooing her. One could imagine that he totally swept her off her feet.

For both Karin and her friends, their summer and autumn in Grez changed them. While Karin fell in love with Carl and he with her, Eva Bonnier entered into an unhappy love affair with sculptor Per Hasselberg (1850–1894). He left her without a backward glance and, following the demise of the relationship, she suffered the first of her debilitating depressions. But that did not stop her, when he died from drinking and hard living at the age of 44, from taking care of his little daughter, Julia, who became like her own daughter. Eva was frequently frustrated by her chosen profession and often felt that she encountered envy and viciousness because she was the rare privileged artist. Most others lived hand-to-mouth.[14]

Even after she recovered from her broken love affair and depression, Eva remained openly critical of Karin's relationship with Carl. Perhaps she was jealous of their love, as her own relationship did not have a happy ending. However, it might have been that she was observant enough to see that Karin was looking a little "battered" back in Paris.[15]

Eva spent a great deal of time with Karin and Carl that winter of 1882 and the beginning of 1883. Karin and Carl's first Christmas Eve in Paris was spent with Eva. She thought that Carl was conceited and that he treated Karin in an exacting and careless way. Karin began looking over cookbooks, according to Eva, while seemingly untroubled by Carl's debts and inability at the time to make the kind of money that Karin's father provided for her— Adolf being the example of what a husband and/or father should provide. She had no help, no bed or desk for herself, and her tasks included washing dishes for Carl—can a woman ask for anything better, Eva is reputed to have written sarcastically in a letter home.[16]

Julia was less interested in men and romance, although she did have a relationship with Spada. However, her primary desire, more than ever after Grez, was to concentrate on landscape painting. And so she left Paris and went back to Grez several times. She eventually ended up living in France permanently—only returning to Sweden infrequently. She did not seem to have a romantic life, concentrating exclusively on her art.[17]

While it must have been edifying for Karin to have been accepted as a student by Alfred Stevens, it was getting letters from Carl when he was in Grez that seemed to mean the most to her.

> How have I waited and looked after your letter. I had already been looking the day before yesterday…. You know what? You are really a great egotist; you think that I have more fun than you? I have not the power like you, running around the mountains and hills; I crawl up into my bed and put my head under the pillow…. The grinding maidens here residing in Colarossi (where I write this) wonder what it is about me, I sit and grin and blow my nose which echoes in the hall. I did receive your letter when I went home. On the stairs, I read "my dear friend," then in the street on my way to Luxembourg, where I read the front page. In this way, I thought you might have followed me and spoke to me…. You say go and speak loudly and imagine that I hear what you say, sure I do, I'm always all the time with you…. Your Karin.[18]

Karin stayed only a few more months in Paris. While despite troubles or trauma both her friends, Eva and Julia, remained artists in France, Karin returned to Hallsberg to prepare for her wedding by stitching towels and bedding and other items that young women of a certain station required for their trousseau.[19] The garments that she made were nothing like what she would create later on in life; she stitched ordinary bridal material such as hemmed bedsheets and pillow cases, a simple table runner sewed by hand, and coverings for bureaus and chests that would give her a start for her new life.

The wedding took place on June 21, 1883, at the Adolf Fredrik Church where Karin had been confirmed into the Lutheran faith 16 years earlier. On both occasions it was the minister, Karl Staaff, who officiated. Sometime after the ceremony, Carl painted her portrait as a bride, showing her wearing a long white gown with a bustle and a modest train. The virginal white dress has long sleeves, a low waist, and a high-necked collar. Carl has her posed in a verdant glen, and she is holding a garland for her hair. She looks young and serious but not unhappy. If his portrait of her is accurate, she was a beautiful bride.[20]

Carl wrote about this painting: "I posed her in her bridal finery, my young wife, right there in the center of the spot on earth where for the first time I had felt happy and where my artistic talent had shown its first bud on a hitherto dormant plant."[21]

This painting was a traditional composition, but sweet and more fanciful than his other watercolors, according to Cavalli-Björkman, who wrote that this picture marked the initiation of Carl into his extensive series of family pictures.[22]

At the wedding were Karin's sister and brother, mother and father (naturally), grandmother, aunts and cousins, along with Carl's mother and father, of whom Carl remarked, "I will never forget the manner in which they [Karin's parents] include my parents in their own social group as well as that of their family. By the way, my parents managed fine. And why wouldn't they? My father truly has what one called a 'good head.' Although he did not know how to use it, and my mother possessed a natural nobility and style, which one does not commonly find in the areas where the poor have their abodes."[23] And indeed Johanna Larsson, Carl's mother, had written Karin a gracious and welcoming letter from Stockholm following the engagement of her son.[24]

During the wedding ceremony, the groom, seemingly overcome with his good fortune, cried and almost dropped the ring. He was 30 and the bride was 23. She was still shy and wide-eyed, and, while fun-loving and even given to a practical joke or two, serious about life and her life's work as a painter. Yes, she had supposedly conquered the most popular member of the artists' colony, the life of every party, but even then Karin was aware that Carl did not come into this marriage, into this relationship, without baggage; he came with his deep well of insecurity and his impoverished and despairing childhood. But he carried excitement and great promise with him as well, for it seems as if Karin knew that he had it in him to become a great painter.

Following the wedding, the couple returned to Grez, where they were festively received by the entire village. Everyone had been impressed with

This portrait completed by Carl shows Karin in her wedding dress, once they were back in Grez following their wedding in Stockholm. Nationalmuseum (Stockholm)/Wikimedia Sverige.

Karin's gentle nature and Carl's commanding leadership when they were there the summer before, so when they returned as bride and groom, the entire colony was ready to celebrate and embrace the couple.

There were fireworks, a regatta on the river with Bengal lights, singing, and music. The Laurents, rather than Madame Chevillon, held a dinner for everyone "to gastronomic heights. Punch bowl! Dancing! The bowl containing everything and anything, and the dances from all around the globe—Indian dances accompanied by the banjo, 'hambopolski,' 'shottis,' and a sweet Apache waltz."[25]

But Carl was there to work. This time he was determined to establish himself once and for all as a serious artist—not just as an illustrator. A significant step in this direction occurred when his painting, *Mère Morot*, was purchased sight-unseen by the influential Swedish collector, Pontus Fürstenberg. Fürstenberg had heard rumblings of Carl Larsson's changed approach to art and, after Carl won the third place medal at the Salon de Paris that first year of his marriage, Fürstenberg knew that he needed to purchase Carl's paintings for his own gallery.

Fürstenberg, the owner of a textile company in Gothenburg, along with his father, became interested in art around 1860, basically giving up his profession to concentrate on starting a career as an art critic and art merchant. Due to a fortuitous marriage to an extremely wealthy heiress, Fürstenberg was able to shift his focus to art-collecting.

He would become Carl's patron for many years.

While Carl was pursuing his dream, Karin was consumed with being a wife. She had stopped working on her art and instead struggled to learn how to cook and keep house. She was frequently in tears over not knowing how to do things around the house. After all, her experience in housewifery was limited. She had never really engaged in domestic tasks, except for the time she was living in Stockholm with the Italian acting family, the Draghis. And there she was not expected to prepare meals, shop, keep house, or generally be responsible for the home; she only had to see to the children and their needs. While she liked to sometimes dabble in the kitchen, making fancy drinks like eggnog or baking gingersnap cookies with her girlfriends, she had never had to prepare three meals a day and maintain a home.

In the beginning, the young couple stayed with Madame Chevillon, but they soon rented a small house located in the guesthouse area of Grez, a place with large windows in the studio. Madame Chevillon had given them some furniture as they had not much more than a few Chinese fans. As Karin by then was responsible for their home furnishings—Carl loved to show off his wife and new home—she had to find suitable furniture, chairs and tables, and cutlery and dishes for entertaining. Since he frequently brought people to the house, Karin struggled with how to prepare meals for a crowd and to entertain. She asked her mother for ideas and for cookbooks, and for Hilda's special recipes. Karin made herring rolls with sweet and sour sauce. But once again her friend, Eva, was not impressed. She described Karin as fumbling, clumsy, and tearful at the beginning of the marriage.[26]

While Karin publicly expressed delight in giving up the artist's life, she may have been at least partially influenced to do so because of the disparaging way in which Carl openly referred to women who painted. He never believed that women should be artists, and he made no secret of this. And then in Grez, several months following her wedding, Karin found herself pregnant. Hilda and Adolf came to visit them. It was the plan that Hilda would assist her daughter when she delivered her first child—and Hilda's first grandchild—but Hilda became, according to Carl, utterly nervous and returned home. Karin and Carl seemed to be a happy couple and were delighted with the pregnancy.

Carl wrote about the momentous hours preceding the birth of their first child: "On August 10 [1884], I asked Paul Chevillon [the innkeeper at the Chevillon hotel in Grez] to drive me to Marlotte, where the midwife lived, and bring her to us. She was a sour-faced octogenarian farmwife. When the old woman had seen and examined Karin she immediately wanted to go back home, but I calmly kept her where she was, despite her vicious protest. In the morning Suzanne arrived and was given that name for the calendar day."[27]

Karin wrote to her parents about the birth: "Your daughter has not been able to be happier than she is now. All has gone so well. Carl so happy.... Her hands are so beautiful, just like her father's.... You should have seen Carl, he cried, 'A girl. A girl.' He knelt at my bed and I almost think he sobbed in joy."[28]

After Suzanne was born, Karin continued to find housewifely duties troublesome. And she still could not cook. She continued writing letters to her mother, asking for help in the form of recipes and other advice. She did not like keeping house. Yet it was following her daughter's birth that Karin finally gave up all attempts to be an artist—putting aside her brushes and watercolors.

Perhaps Karin made the correct choice. Members of Karin's family have said that she "willingly gave up painting after searching her heart."[29] At the time, she must have recognized how difficult it would be as an unmarried female artist in France and in Sweden, and how almost impossible it would have been to be married to someone like Carl and continue to paint— and perhaps even compete against each other. Karin was always a dreamer, but with a realistic streak. She knew what she wanted and she knew how to get it: badgering her parents to move from the French School to the Arts and Crafts School, getting into the Royal Academy, moving to Paris to study—and perhaps even wooing Carl away from other women in Grez, who in all probability found him charming, dynamic, and exciting.

Maybe after all it had been Karin doing the wooing—not Carl.

Could she have been a great artist? She did have talent as evidenced by her paintings. Most did not survive, but the few that did, the ones she worked on during her student years in Paris and Grez, showed that she was gifted in terms of the use of color. These gifts would again come to the fore later in her life.

So now, instead of an artist, Karin became an art critic. She was not only Carl's wife, mother of his daughter, and his model, she would also become the best reviewer of his work—his muse and inspiration.

As for Carl, the marriage swept him into the affluent middle class for the first time in his life. With Fürstenberg as his patron, with the new style of painting that Carl now embraced, with medals finally received from the Salon de Paris, and with the security of a wealthy and accepting family behind him, Carl's life had clearly changed for the better.

As will be shown, working under Karin's direction, Carl became one of Sweden's most beloved artists. He will be viewed as the patriarch of a wonderful family and he will become wealthy from his own earnings for the first time in his life.

You might say that, with Karin as his muse, his life and his work became her mission and his glory.

8

The Mother, 1884–1888

Carl Larsson's painting *A Studio Idyll* depicts his one-year-old daughter, Suzanne, seated on the lap of her mother, Karin—both on a chair in their rented Paris apartment. Karin is staring straight ahead looking at the artist—a pose that she did not often take. Sleepy Suzanne reclines on her breast. Karin appears serene and calm and is dressed in the formal Parisian way of a woman of her stature. She wears a high-necked gray dress, with a brooch closing the lace collar. Her hair is back in a bun, with tendrils falling on each side of her face. Carl has placed Karin in the center of the picture, with the child at the bottom right-hand corner, almost out of the frame. Baby Suzanne's hair is blonde and tousled and she, too, seems to be looking with half-closed eyes at her father, the painter. Karin, in Carl's portraits, generally gives the impression of being at peace, content with her situation in life.

This type of painting was an aberration for Carl. His aim was to paint great murals, not family portraits, which he did just to keep his wife happy.

By the time he died, however, two-thirds of Carl's work would involve his family. His works would hang in Stockholm's Nationalmuseum and the Gothenburg Museum, as well as in other countries of the world, including the United States. Karin, along with Suzanne and her six surviving children, would in time become famous all over the world—not as an artist, but as the subject of her husband's art. However, during these early years of their marriage and family life, such portraits would be minimal as Carl was more focused on working on landscapes from around Grez. As for Karin, when she wasn't sitting for a painting, she continued to put her indomitable spirit and extraordinary energy into being the perfect housewife, mother, and handler. Karin needed all her serenity to keep up with her husband, as living with him was often a challenge. Carl could be like a boiling volcano or a restless sprit, swinging from one extreme to the other. Sometimes he could be smiling, dynamic, and personable, but at other times he was desperate and throwing his palette against the wall.[1]

81

This portrait by Carl of his wife and firstborn child, Suzanne, was completed while the family was living in Paris. Nationalmuseum (Stockholm)/Wikimedia Sverige.

While Carl was painting furiously, Karin continued to learn how to cook and to entertain their many Grez visitors. They included Eva Bonnier and her sister; August Strindberg; Christian Skredavig (1854–1924), a Norwegian painter and writer; and his wife, Maggie Plahte. They were also visited by Tekla Lindeström (1856–1937), an engraver, who was married to Carl's good friend, Karl Nordström. Karin's parents, Hilda and Adolf, along with siblings Per and Stina, also came frequently.

Of course they also saw much of Julia Beck, who was also working at Grez. She was frequently accompanied by her lover, Johan Christian Janzon (1853–1910), who was a foreign correspondent for the *Stockholm Dagblot*; he used the moniker "Spada" (sword) to commemorate his military service and his activities as a war correspondent. Spada was a close friend of Carl's.[2,3]

Karin's anxiety about hosting all these visitors, both at Grez and later in Paris, belied her serene expression in Carl's portrait of her with Suzanne. In a letter to her mother from Grez on September 7, 1883, she wrote: "Oh my mother pray for me! Strindberg comes here! Eva Bonnier and her sister will be here any day. Also a Mr and Mrs Skredavig came for a few days. His wife was enchanting, cute, witty, and talented. How do you think I should behave with such a collection of people? Do you think Carl will be ashamed for me? You write that I should try to be natural. But it is precisely the art of being there, when I get so embarrassed that my limbs solidify. You lose what little banter you have. My heart is in my throat when I talk."[4]

Karin relished the role of mother and loved taking care of Suzanne. It has been said that the infant was the first non–Grez, or non–French-born, baby in the village and so became a double celebrity: model for her father and town novelty, with many of the villagers wanting to see this foreign little girl. Karin was a willing learner, getting cooking hints from her mother and from the women in Grez, who showed her how to cook delicious French provincial recipes that she would use later when entertaining the leading lights of Sweden's artistic and literary community. She also held four o'clock tea parties in Grez, likely so as to fend off loneliness. She was left alone a great deal, as Carl only surfaced when it was time for meals, coffee, or brandy.

Carl was thrilled with how well Karin was learning to be a housewife and a *femme d'artiste* (wife of an artist). He was full of admiration for her cooking, particularly her ragout, omelets, muffins, onion and vegetable soups, and fruit compotes. Mother Hilda, however, worried that Karin did not have an outlet for her art. Carl's response to Hilda was that Karin now had important work, for she was the one empowering his work.[5]

Carl had a firm trust and belief in the good "eye" Karin had for what he was working on, for his use of color and his style. He came to rely on her instincts for what was good and what was not so good. He understood that she knew art and art-making and what an audience might want and like. And nothing, no painting, was signed off on without Karin's consent and approval.[6]

The arrangement between them solidified: Karin could not paint, but she could mentor Carl, model for him, act as hostess, and raise his children. She was also a live-in psychiatrist because she frequently helped Carl dispel his moods and disappointments. But Karin's life was not all work. Almost the entire Swedish art community was in residence in Grez. There were many parties, especially around the holidays: Spada sang, several women singers from Sweden performed nightly, pianos were played in all the boarding houses and hotels, and masked balls abounded.

Following Suzanne's birth the new family stayed in Grez for nine months. They then went back to Sweden, in spite of the efforts of the French government to convince Carl to stay in France. As Carl was becoming increasingly well-regarded, he had finally become a favored son of the Parisian art set. But he was anxious to use the techniques from Grez—outdoor painting, nature presented realistically—back in his own country.

Carl had debated living in Paris as at that time he held his native land in disdain, as did many of the Grez artists, because of its treatment of creative people. But he also held a deep-seated and almost unconscious attachment to Sweden, and the pull to return was great. One can only assume that Karin wanted to go back home to be with her family, especially her mother, now that she was married and had a child.

Everything seemed to be working in favor of the couple returning to Stockholm. In the autumn of 1885, Karin and Carl made the decision to provide Hilda with rented living space in the city. She settled into a two-flights-up spacious flat where everyone could have their own room, as Stina was still a schoolgirl and needed a quiet place to study. Brother Per was back in Hallsberg, learning his father's business. Hilda was also a great hostess and entertained not only her family but business colleagues of her husband and Karin and Carl's artist friends as well.

Later Hilda moved to a larger space on Linnegata 5, with Carl, Karin, and baby Suzanne joining her. Adolf was infrequently in Stockholm, staying in Hallsberg or traveling elsewhere for business. Shortly thereafter they all moved to an even larger residence at Nybrogatan 47 in Östermalm, which was then and is still now one of Stockholm's most exclusive addresses. The area is home to huge five- and six-story mansions and a large park, Humlegården, where outdoor theatre performances took place in the summer. Close to Hilda's home was the wonderful Saluhall, a food market constructed in 1889 of brick on a cast-iron frame with turrets and pinnacles, vaulted windows, and considerable ornamentation. One can imagine Karin and her mother strolling and chatting with their food baskets on their arms while shopping for dinner there.[7]

Back in Stockholm Karin had her mother to help with Suzanne—providing her with more time to cater to Carl, both his art and his whims. When he was not painting outside, he would urge Karin to sit for him for hours as he painted or sketched one scene after another of family life. And if he met someone on the street or read something in a newspaper article that expressed a negative view of him or his work, he would become furious, forcing Karin to smooth out his ruffled feathers and dampen his angry outbursts.

She would also be Carl's traveling companion, leaving her child behind, as she accompanied her husband to Gothenburg and back and forth to Paris. During 1885 Carl continued with his experiments: trying to figure out how he wanted to paint, what he wanted to paint, and why he wanted to paint, although he found the idea of plein air painting intriguing. But his real desire was to be a muralist. So he needed to travel throughout Europe—Venice, Rome, Messina—where he studied murals. Carl also examined Michelangelo and Tiepolo, artists who would influence his work. Often Karin went with him.

This would become part of a pattern: Karin's parents, especially Hilda, would take care of the children while Karin traveled with Carl. Carl, especially in the early years, did not want to be away from his wife—his support, his confidante, his solace, and his advocate.

During the summer of 1885, Carl took a trip with Karin's father to Dalarna to visit Karin's two aunts, Maria and Ulla, who lived in a small cottage that once belonged to their mother. Carl was impressed with the area: the beautiful countryside and the rural attractiveness of the landscape. Dalarna reminded Carl of Grez, one of the places he was happiest, and he wanted Karin to come and see the area to which she had not returned since she was a girl.

Adolf offered to buy him a cottage, but Carl turned him down. According to Karin's Swedish biographer, Carl was not yet ready to settle down in the country; he was actually planning to go back to Grez. At some point, however, he did bring Karin back to Sundborn.

One September day while with Suzanne, Karin knelt down on the bridge over the Sundborn creek. "No indeed!" she cried. Carl had not exaggerated. With its yellow birches, meadows, fields, and creek, not to mention its village hospitality, Sundborn could be a wonderful place for them. Karin wrote to her parents following her visit: "This is so fervently good. Suzanne has been making great progress. I am so happy that the aunts are happy. I think we were really welcome. And Aunt Ulla is so hearty and surprisingly, one would not think that she was so ill."[8]

But Karin knew that Carl was not ready for rural life, no matter how appealing.

Although the young family first resided with Karin's mother in Stockholm, they wanted a place of their own. They eventually found a small flat on Åsögatan, a street in the current Södermalm district in Stockholm. They lived on a block of flats consisting of small red cabins that had been built in the 1700s. Their new cottage had a garden, a tiny kitchen that also served as a library, a small room for Carl's "painting paraphernalia," a study that functioned as a dining room, and a bedroom upstairs. They also had a serving girl, Lotta, who was brought over from Hilda's household, and who had quite the temper. She established herself immediately and made it known that she was not happy to be dealing with such poor people as Carl and Karin, used as she was to living under the direction of Hilda Bergöö. But, as Carl wrote, it was "mighty decent" for someone who was used to better to stick with them for several years. Actually, she was honest and reliable, took over the household, and, under Hilda's tutelage, learned to be a great cook. Lotta certainly made Karin's life easier, as she relieved her of that which she was not thrilled to be doing—housewifely duties.[9]

Now that they were back in Sweden, Nordic weather somewhat hampered Carl's experiments in this new plein air technique. Painting in a Stockholm winter was not quite as desirable as painting in a sunny French countryside in spring and summer. Carl painted one picture depicting a poor Swedish artist, muffled to his ears, painting in the snow, with footprints indicating people stopping to watch the crazy but determined outdoor painter.

Regardless of the very real impediments of weather as well as the social climate, Carl was developing a following using watercolors, which he applied in a singular way—he first outlined his figures in black and then continued painting using vibrant colors. This outlining made the images he was painting stand out more. He also used his imagination to create storylines for his paintings, using models in various poses that illustrated the plot.

Now back in Stockholm, both Carl and Karin took up again with the group of innovative literati, the Opponents, renamed the Artists Association. The Association continued its fight with the administration of the Royal Academy that had begun years ago. Artists, especially those coming back to Sweden from France, felt that the Academy's courses were not progressive enough and did not include ideas and techniques coming out of places like the artists' colony in Grez.

Karin continued to become an increasingly more sophisticated hostess for her husband. With the help of Lotta, she was now recreating the wonderful dishes from the old women in Grez. She made French soup, using leeks as well as onions. She learned how to make bread and black currant jelly. She cooked dishes that were not common in Sweden such as polenta, bean pudding, pastas and other Italian foods she remembered from her time living with the Draghi family.

Carl continued agitating the Royal Academy to make changes in its way of teaching artists, which had not altered since the seventeenth century. And there were also concerns with how the government viewed artists and the sale of domestic artwork, which was taxed and heavily regulated in a way that was not in the artist's favor. The Association wrote a strongly worded letter to the Academy, putting forth their criticisms and suggestions for making artists' lives easier and the purchase of art less cumbersome. They not only wanted to change the antiquated curricula from one based on Roman and Greek theories to one that concentrated on more day-to-day activities, but they also wanted the restrictions levied on women to be lifted.[10]

There was much turmoil on Swedish college and university campuses as well. As far back as 1882, for example, students from Uppsala University, the premier institution of higher learning in Sweden, established the Verdandi, a club that supported progressive literati, inviting speakers and lecturers who wanted to overturn art and literature curricula all over Sweden.[11]

This agitation was brought back from Paris by female artists from Karin's own circle. Considered the intellectual elite, women who had known each other since childhood, such as Hanna Hirsch (who would become Hanna Pauli), Julia Beck, and Eva Bonnier, all worked to change the academic system for artists. They had been tutored by feminist philosopher Ellen Key (1849–1926), who would be one of the writers to tout Karin Larsson in the coming years, depicting her as both muse to her husband but, more importantly, as a design force in her own right.[12]

At this time in Sweden, and especially in Stockholm, there were few galleries or art exhibitions. Intellectuals and artists relied on "readings, lectures, musical performance, the theatre" for their social lives and as a way of displaying their art. More contemporary art ideas and concepts were not introduced into the academic curricula. Artists and students had to go out into the world for their inspiration and art theory.[13]

During April of 1885, a huge juried exhibition was held at Blanch's Art Salon on the Kungsträdgården, a large park in central Stockholm. This show, entitled *Från Seinens strand* (From the Banks of the Seine), included more than 100 artists, including Carl Larsson, Georg Pauli, Anders Zorn, and others. It was diametrically opposed to what was popular in Swedish art at the time, which was studio art done in dark gloomy oils with the model in the studio rather than out in the world. The prevailing style was studied poses in a static portrayal instead of something with more narrative force. Carl exhibited seven works, which included eighteenth-century costume pieces, one of which was *The Vines*, an outdoor painting with a woman at its center in an elaborate gown. He had not yet begun in earnest to paint his family, with the exception of those few small portraits of Karin and Suzanne discussed earlier. He was instead helping to create a movement in Sweden, the National Romantic painters, which was a driving political force whose proponents included Georg Pauli, Nils Kreuger, Karl Nordström, Prince Eugen, with Carl as more or less the standard-bearer. These painters considered themselves the wise men who penetrated mysteries of nature and nation, and revealed them to the Swedish public.[14]

Carl's quest for fame and credibility meant that he traveled wherever opportunities presented themselves. When Karin stayed in Stockholm, they wrote many letters back and forth, and Karin still lamented the long waits for replies. In March 1886 she wrote, "Wednesday. Now I have you on board the steamer to Copenhagen, munching smoked salmon, lobster, shrimp…. I have followed you all night…. Thursday, Friday, Saturday. No letter…. I sit in my bed at six on Sunday morning and write (could not resist). Suzanne has been on my arm, now and then looked up with one eye, thumbed me in the face with her little fingers and kissed me on the cheek or where she arrived at. The sweetest baby in the world!"[15]

Carl continued to work on commissioned pieces, especially for Pontus Fürstenberg. With the help of his patron, Carl was appointed as head of the Gothenburg Museum Drawing School in Valand. The Valand School of Fine Art, as it was called, was founded as Göteborgs Musei Ritskola (Gothenburg Museum Drawing School) in 1865, and has been part of the University of Gothenburg since 1977. Valand was the name of the construction company formed in order to build the original building that is now occupied by a nightclub of the same name. At first Karin stayed in Stockholm while Carl went on ahead to Valand in August 1886. She made the move with Suzanne to join him a few months later. Gothenburg, the second largest city in Sweden, is on the west coast on the North Sea. It was then and is today a student town. It's unclear how much culture was there for Karin to enjoy, and surely she missed her mother, who had been a great help in looking after Suzanne, but just being with her family was wonderful for Karin.

They moved into a house owned by Fürstenberg outside the city, which Carl liked very much, although it seems that Karin was not thrilled about the move. Nonetheless she managed to decorate their living space by putting up curtains and making spaces for his old books and a good place for Suzanne to sleep.[16]

Karin wrote to her mother that Carl took his teaching responsibilities very seriously. When Carl first arrived at the school, it was little more than a finishing school for young women who wanted to dabble in art. He changed all that, transforming it into a "painter school," and allowed the students to use a live model, which created a terrible scandal in the decorous city.

He wrote about these female students in a way that reinforced his disdain for female artists: "When I write about the school, I have to talk about its students. I inherited most of them from the old school—semi-old married women, who probably had fooled their husbands into believing they had some talent, when in fact they were too lazy to take care of their households, and then young daughters of the rich, who were seeking a pastime and wanted to impress their girl friends."[17]

During this time Karin was probably not too happy. Carl, as always, was focused on his own life and even wrote that he spent a great deal of time away from her, partying. She was also pregnant again. This pregnancy was much more difficult than with Suzanne, and with Carl returning home in the wee hours of the morning, how could it have been a good time for her?

It was perhaps early one morning, rather than late one night, when Carl wrote, "and as I puffed my way up the Victoria Hill I saw lights in the windows."[18] Carl, knowing that the birth was imminent because of these early morning lights, ran to get the midwife, a Mrs. Hanson, after which he knelt by Karin's bed all day. It was not until evening on April 4, 1887, that Ulf, their son, was born.

During their years in Gothenburg, Karin and Carl resided at Apelviken in Varberg during the summer, where Karin had lived a whole summer during her Royal Academy days. They were accompanied by Karin's younger sister, Stina. These were lovely times. Suzanne was happy to be with her Aunt Stina and loved the countryside. Little Ulf nuzzled at his mother's breast, and everyone enjoyed the swimming and the surf. And Karin was happy. She wrote to her mother saying that she was thrilled that Carl was home for dinner and that they now could enjoy long, pleasant evenings. She wrote, "Carl has (knock on wood) not been too much on parties."[19]

The cottage was charming: it had an outside wall and stone fencing enclosing the orchard. It was a lovely little cottage by the sea where they could bathe naked if they wanted to.

Carl was still working in oils, now painting murals for Fürstenberg. During this time he was also painting landscapes of Sweden in watercolors and working actively as an illustrator in order to make money for his family. His artistic personality was somewhat conflicted. He still yearned to be recognized as a historic muralist. When Fürstenberg built his new palace at Brunnsparken in Gothenburg, Carl was commissioned to adorn the top-floor gallery with three monumental paintings in the allegorical form, envisioning the development of art. It was his first major contribution to the genre, and he succeeded beyond expectations. Carl focused on narratives from the Renaissance, the Rococo period, and Modern Art, which he depicted "with more good humor than monumental feeling."[20]

In 1888, while working on Fürstenberg's mural, Carl entered a contest to create frescos for the Nationalmuseum, Stockholm and northern Europe's most prestigious art museum. For many years Swedes wanted to see the great expanse of walls in the museum's stairwell decorated. For many artists, being offered the commission to create murals for the museum was their dream, their primary goal. Years back when Carl was still in Grez, a similar competition had been announced. Carl had submitted a proposal but was rejected. Now, he wrote to Fürstenberg, he was ready to submit another proposal, which he did anonymously with the motto "Everything for the Fatherland." It would be some years before Carl was considered for this commission, and it would be one of the worst experiences of his life.

During this time of feverish activity by Carl, Karin was taking care of two small children in a city that she was unfamiliar with. And the children and Carl were not always doing so well: Ulf had trouble with his diet, Suzanne was a toddler who was constantly running around and missing her grandmother, and Carl was beginning to experience severe headaches. It was only when Stina came for a visit from Stockholm that Karin felt happy. Stina helped with the children, of course, but more importantly she was a companion to Karin, who was often alone.

Karin was so busy with childcare and domestic duties that she had little time to mentor Carl or even pose for him. Additionally, all of his attention was on other types of paintings: oils especially, which Karin was not very fond of.

At this point Carl was getting somewhat bored in Gothenburg, and perhaps Karin was, too. Carl persuaded Fürstenberg to allow him to complete the paintings he was working on for him in Paris. These paintings were to be the basis for a private art gallery that would eventually become the Gothenburg Museum of Art. In order to do this, Carl would have to hand over the reins of the school to someone else, which he did. He then had to convince Karin to come with him. He frequently refused to travel without his wife. Thus he and Karin returned together to Paris where they lived for a year, leaving Suzanne and Ulf at home in Hallsberg with the in-laws and Lotta.

Little is mentioned about Karin's feelings on leaving her children. Surely she felt that they would be well taken care of by her mother—by all accounts a wonderful grandmother. And Karin knew that Carl's need for her was great. While she was not very involved in his art-making at this time, she was always his comforting ally, his soother, and his best critic. Whatever her feelings, she likely had no choice in the matter. Carl, it seemed, was always her first priority.

It was while they were in Paris and Carl was working on Fürstenberg's murals for his home that their third child, Pontus, was born on October 26, 1888.

Carl admitted that he had no time for this new baby—or for the other two children, either. He recalled that Pontus was somewhat obstinate and blunt, perhaps because he saw little of his father who was busy getting ready for the Paris World's Fair in 1889, where he was planning on exhibiting a number of paintings. This took up all his time and energy.

Carl was more determined than ever to achieve success.

No doubt Karin felt lonely, having been left to her own devices in a city that she once loved. It must have been a very unpleasant time for her without her two little children and her newborn, and again a missing husband with no family nearby. While Carl was off in the countryside painting in the open air and out in the evenings with friends, she was adrift. Carl was using live models; one was a blonde woman he worked with while in Grez. One wonders how Karin felt about her husband using these women as models for his paintings, some of which were nudes. By all accounts Carl was never interested in any other woman once he met Karin, so perhaps she was reasonably sure that he was faithful to her—all mentions of their marriage indicated that Carl was faithful and Karin had an understanding of his work. There was never any hint of scandal or promiscuity on Carl's part.

They had a meager budget provided by Fürstenberg, so as a family they were living frugally. Somehow, however, Carl himself managed to live in a grand style—with parties at home and treats for friends, which Fürstenberg apparently paid for in addition to the salary he was paying him for the three murals. It can be assumed that Karin, always thrifty, managed the funds so that Carl could be expansive when he needed to be.

They also went back and forth to Grez while living in Paris, but most of their friends, Spada, Pauli, and others, were no longer there, so they never stayed long.

This photograph of Karin with the newest child, Pontus, was taken in 1888 shortly after Pontus' birth while Carl and Karin were living in Paris. This photograph has been provided by the Carl Larsson-Gården, Sundborn, Sweden, and is used with permission.

While they were in Paris, Karin's Aunt Ulla died. She was living with her sister, Maria, in the small cottage called Lilla Hyttnäs. Since Maria did not want to live there alone, Adolf gave the small, run-down cottage to Karin and Carl as a gift, asking only that they put money into an account for their children's education in lieu of payment for the home.

This dwelling was to change the trajectory of Carl's painting, making the family not only wealthy but famous in Sweden and Germany. But, more importantly, it would provide Karin with an outlet for her art that had lain dormant for five years. It would be here in Sundborn where Karin would reinvent herself as an artist.

She and her family would not live there permanently for a few more years; they would continue to live in Stockholm, traveling to their new, somewhat run-down cottage in the summer. This home was to be their vacation villa.

9

The Cottage, 1889–1890

Carl and Karin, with Pontus Robert August, their newly born baby (his middle name after the husband of the midwife, Madame Hiltz),[1] returned once again to Sweden by ship in the summer of 1889 to reunite with Suzanne and Ulf in Hallsberg. One can only imagine how joyful it must have been for Karin to return to not only her two children but also her parents. But the return must have been difficult as well—one year without her children! Ulf, who was so little when the couple left him with his grandparents, called his father "uncle."[2]

The stay in Paris and the confinement with Pontus had been troublesome for Karin. She was frequently alone and often not well, suffering from pneumonia and bronchitis. A psychologist might make a connection between her aborted artistic career, three pregnancies, and an absent husband with some of her maladies.

Carl felt that certain activities were necessary to sustain him, such as horseback riding, keeping in touch with his Nordic artist friends, painting out in the countryside, and making frequent return trips to Sweden. And while they may have been necessary, they did leave Karin alone. But it was not in Karin's nature to complain. She always did what she had to do, following her own conscience, as an independent thinker. From her days at the Royal Academy where she had been surrounded by forward-thinking women, she had made her mark, which was typical of women of her time and social class—women like Eva Bonnier and Julia Beck who did not accept men as "leaders" of their families. Karin, as a product of an independent mother, was used to bucking the norm, making a conscious choice not to complain. Perhaps this trait then is not unusual for someone like Karin.

It is true that she did accompany Carl on a few trips while they were in Paris, and she must have found satisfaction in advising Carl on his commissions and his work. But Karin had no art of her own to concentrate on and her two children were being raised by her mother and father mainly because Carl hated to be parted from her.

Their stay in Hallsberg was short, but while there Carl became engaged in painting murals on the walls of the upstairs apartment for his in-laws' new home. Perhaps Karin even had some say in the content of the murals. This was a harbinger for how life would one day be in their own little cottage.

Adolf, by now very wealthy, wanted to move from the White House in Hallsberg where the family had grown up to a more substantial one in the same area, which is why he commissioned a young architect and designer, someone from Falun, to build him a new home.

Gustav Ferdinand Boberg (1860–1946), who was a year younger than Karin, drew up the plans. Boberg would later become a big name in Swedish architectural history and would soon be one of the country's most sought-after architects. It was Boberg who would build Prince Eugen's Waldemarsudde, one of Sweden's most beautiful art museums. He also designed the Thiel Gallery, as well as churches, fire stations, department stores, and many other buildings in Stockholm and around Sweden.[3]

Having barely finished his training, Boberg's first commission would be Adolf's house. He was another poor boy like Carl and, to some degree, like Adolf himself, who trained as a mechanical engineer. Karin and Boberg were acquainted in Stockholm, having gone to school there at around the same time, which may be why Adolf gave the commission to build his home to the unknown architect.

In order to make the house special, Carl created many murals, especially in the great hall on the second floor where he painted pictures around the top of the room.

It was exciting to be involved in making this new home for Adolf and Hilda beautiful. Carl painted murals along the top of the room called the great hall, which was the formal drawing room. He painted family members, such as Adolf himself and Aunt Lisen.[4]

However much fun it was to help decorate the *Bergööhuset* (Bergöö house), both Carl and Karin were eager to get to Sundborn, to the cottage gift from Adolf that was waiting for them. After about a month in Hallsberg, they made the trip in July 1889. Although living in the small, dilapidated home was a challenge with three little ones, Karin loved the fresh air and the village life. She was delighted to plant a vegetable garden, interact with the villagers, and to finally have the opportunity to all be together as a family for the first time in quite a while.

Lilla Hyttnäs was a cottage that had been in Adolf's family since the death of his father in 1875, at which time Adolf purchased it. The cottage was small, even for his widowed mother and Karin's two aunts, so it would be a very crowded residence for Carl, Karin, the three small children, and

This watercolor of the Sundborn cottage was completed by Carl and was reproduced in his book, *A Hom*. Nationalmuseum (Stockholm)/Wikimedia Sverige.

any help they might bring in. The home had three rooms on the ground and first floors, with an extension of sorts in the front that contained the entrance hall and stairs. It also had a lean-to on one side of the building.[5]

As they had been a somewhat itinerant family for many years, renting flats in Gothenburg, Stockholm, Paris, and Grez, and living in furnished spaces or hotel rooms, they had little to bring to the new dwelling. The rooms were small and in poor repair, and the grounds surrounding the house, while beautiful, were unkept and the ground was not ready for flowers and vegetable gardens. The two aunts who had lived there were not up to doing any work on the cottage, so Karin would have her work cut out for her, both inside and outside the house. She was thrilled with the challenge, however, of making the run-down cottage a home for her family, and Carl was delighted to finally have a real home of his own. In addition to the renovations of the cottage itself, Karin also took it upon herself to renew the leftover furniture, which included fine Gustavian pieces that needed to be spruced up.

Life in the little country village was going to be a different experience for Karin. This would be a far cry from her family's home and life in Paris or Stockholm. Paris, of course, was Paris—a beautiful city filled with artists and cosmopolitan residents, spacious boulevards, and delightful parks. But

This watercolor, *A Day of Celebration*, was painted by Carl Larsson. It depicts the children dressed in costume to celebrate the name day of their maid, Emma. They had been decorated by Karin and show her designed textiles. The ceiling is uniquely hung with material of red stripes and embroidered birds. Nationalmuseum (Stockholm)/Wikimedia Sverige.

given Karin's loneliness there, she did not have fond memories of her most recent stay in the city. And they had no home of their own in France, either in Paris or Grez.

Stockholm, where they lived off and on, was crowded, with a widening gap between rich and poor. There were trams running through the streets and masses of farmers coming to the capital looking to make a decent living. Even though many of Sweden's citizens had fled to America, many more flooded the major Swedish cities looking for work. Yes, there were beautiful buildings in Stockholm designed by famous architects such as Fredrik Lilljekvist. (Boberg would not begin designing buildings in Stockholm until several years later.) And yes, there was the Royal Swedish Academy of Fine Arts. But there was polluted air and the stench of sewage, and ghettos were set throughout the city. Politically, only the rich had options and voting rights; the poor and women were not yet eligible to vote.[6] But Sundborn had fresh air and clean water running through the creek beside the cottage.

And the villagers did not seem to realize that women were disenfranchised as they had work within the village, and, while not wealthy by any stretch of the imagination, the men and women of Sundborn were farmers, carpenters, woodworkers, and other repair people who were all about earning their daily living without thinking about being deprived.

Gothenburg, the other city where the family spent time, was not much better than Stockholm. During the Swedish emigration to the United States in the nineteenth and early twentieth centuries, about 1.3 million Swedes left the country via Gothenburg to Hull, UK. (From there they took a train across Britain to Liverpool and the huge ships that would carry them to New York's harbor.) So Gothenburg was a city in constant motion. The wealthy lived in overdecorated houses and the workers lived in wooden houses in the overpopulated city district, Haga; today tourists view those houses as picturesque, but at the time they were dingy, dirty, and over-crowded.[7] And once again, when Karin and Carl were there, they lived in homes provided by Fürstenburg.

So to Karin, Sundborn must have been idyllic and reminiscent of the wonderful surroundings she lived in with Carl in Grez.

Sundborn maintained a certain provincial calm and contained none of the noise and chaos of the larger cities. And, importantly for the emerging designer inside Karin, Sundborn had carpenters who would interpret her furniture drawings and painters who would help make her artistic visions a reality. For instance, she created a rocking chair—seen today in IKEA's catalogue.[8] However, the chair was considered so ugly—big, bulky, and unappealing—that Karin's carpenter, Mr. Arnbom, was too ashamed to deliver the finished product in daylight. He hauled the chair over to the cottage in the dark of night.[9]

Karin made drawings of the chair and had carpenters in the village make the chair according to her specifications. It was a broad, sturdy, square piece of furniture, unadorned, with a cushioned seat and padded cushion on the back of the chair. It was more than wide enough to hold a mother and child. Its wood construction was strong and it was a piece of furniture that would be utilized for decades, not only by the Larsson family members, but by anyone who bought it from IKEA.

And best of all, while their home in Sundborn was small and over-crowded, it was theirs. The outdoor space, with the possibility of blooming trees, flower and vegetable gardens, and the creek, made the home more spacious than any of their flats in Stockholm and other spaces they had lived in while continuously hosting visiting relatives and famous Scandi-navian artists and writers. The expectations for Karin to be a good hostess and cook would be somewhat lifted here in the country.

This photograph is of the rocking chair that Karin designed and had built that has been copied by IKEA. The photograph is from the collection of the Bergöö home in Hallsberg and is used with permission from Ulrik Jansson.

Even today Sundborn is one of Sweden's loveliest areas, especially in the spring and summer, with its pine trees, brilliant blue lakes, colorful wildflowers, and abundant wildlife. The weather is continental, with cold winters and hot summers (like Minnesota or North Dakota). Karin, often ill in Stockholm, could recuperate in the bracing unpolluted air of the Dalarna province. The children could run unrestrained across the pastures and through the woods and splash about in the Sundborn creek during the warm summers.

In the few years before their move to Sundborn, Carl had become well-known. He was now winning both prizes and commissions and was asked to complete portraits of famous people such as friends Anders Zorn, Selma Lagerlöf, and August Strindberg. But most of his funds came from his Gothenburg patron, as well as a salary for his continued work as director of the Valand Academy, the art school in Gothenburg.

For the first time in their married life, Carl and Karin did not have money problems. They felt they could invest funds into their cottage as

Sundborn would be their summer residence and a haven for their expanding family over the years.

Carl viewed the cottage as his first real home, and indeed it was the first one he owned. He totally embraced the community of Sundborn, writing, "The Sundborners are magnificent people." To commemorate them he painted many portraits of his most favorite neighbors, many of whom helped Karin fix up the cottage, little by little, as Karin and Carl got more money. They could not have completed their cottage without the help of painter Persson, carpenter Arnbom, and blacksmith Erickson. These and others from the village helped to make their cottage habitable, but perhaps more importantly made their residence in the village meaningful and special.[10]

The children seemed to like it in Sundborn, too. Of course it was wonderful to have both parents with them. Suzanne was old enough to run outside and play in the yard and throw stones into the creek. Pontus, the little baby, would be propped up on the floor in his mother's work room watching her sew and draw. Suzanne accused Ulf of being both "clumsy and chubby"; as the oldest sibling, she was used to bossing him around. And old Anna Damberg, the housekeeper, would see to it that they did not fall into the stream.[11]

Their happiness this first summer was so great that Carl even joined the family for church in the village.

But then, of course, Carl started to travel again. And while the family's plan had been to use the Sundborn cottage only as a summer villa, Karin stayed with the children through that first winter while Carl went on to Gothenburg as he continued his association with the Valand Academy a bit longer.

During that autumn, Carl took a trip to Italy with Pontus Fürstenberg and his wife. Then, on a pretext that Rome was being visited by a horrible epidemic, Carl convinced the Fürstenbergs to return to Paris. Once there Carl expressed his desire to return to Sundborn. Apparently this annoyed Fürstenberg. The old man, as Carl called him in his memoir, banged his fist on the table and shouted that Carl only wanted to go home because of this "damned attraction to your wife that is driving you."[12]

Carl also took an autumn trip to Holland and France with architect Carl Möller (1857–1933), a Swedish designer and public official. Carl continued to travel and stay busy, and, in spite of his desire to go home to Sundborn, he was often cranky, exhausted, and ill-tempered on his return there. When Carl overextended himself, he suffered from severe headaches. And he was still unable to take criticism or negative reactions to his paintings. Whenever that happened, he would sulk, leaving it up to Karin to pull him from his doldrums.

The relationship between Carl and Karin was one of a turbulent sea and a cool pond. But was Karin such a calm person, or did she carry within herself an inner tension? According to her Swedish biographer—and son-in-law—Alex Frieberg, she had her anxieties but did not express them like Carl did. Frieberg asked, "Is not the life at the side of a genius strenuous?" How did she deal with his depressions, which were frequent, along with his professional jealousies?[13]

If one of his friends—or enemies—achieved a goal that Carl had set for himself, he would become agitated and upset. On one hand he could show deep affection and gratitude to Karin, and on the other hand his dominant personality could feel like tyranny. How did she handle these conflicts and outbursts? He would sulk and go to his room or wander off into the village, leaving her to her own devices. It was worse in large cities like Paris or Stockholm because Carl would find people to party with there, but in Sundborn, the village was small—Carl could not readily get away from his home as he did in Stockholm. One wonders how or why Karin would put up with Carl's dark moods. Perhaps she thought all men had their weaknesses, or perhaps she was blind to Carl's deficiencies.[14]

Frieberg explains this tension by saying that both Karin and Carl had willpower as well as artistic temperaments—for she was a strong woman, there is no doubt about that. But it seems as if she was able to restrain herself, keeping her frustrations under control, perhaps because of her stable upbringing. She used her willpower to care for Carl, take charge of the children, and look after the home, and she used her physical strength to clear the land around their cottage, eventually creating a bountiful flower and vegetable garden. And once they were established in Sundborn, she began to use her artistic temperament to produce textile creations.[15]

Karin had her own shortcomings, of course. She still had trouble using language, as can be seen in her letters, perhaps because of her still-troubling dyslexia and inability at times to focus. She could be funny and generally very wise—wise in that she had learned as a child to contain her own unhappiness and put a good face on it. Frieberg opines that some of her internal conflicts may have resulted in illnesses of the throat and chest, which possibly suggest some anxiety. Outwardly, however, she was calm. Was she a little sad? No, not sad. She was a serious woman, always had been, but dealt with life with an underlying humor.[16]

In early 1890 Carl continued traveling while Karin happily stayed in Sundborn. In fact, she seemed to mind Carl's absences less now that she was making a real home for her family there.

However, all was not well with the family. Karin's father had been ill for a good bit of his life, and in March his health began to seriously deteriorate.

Carl visited Hilda and Adolf in Stockholm and found that Adolf was not well at all, and that the burden of caring for him worried Hilda and caused her to not feel well either.

At the same time, Carl was having his own setbacks and was miserable, thinking more about his disappointments than about Adolf's ill health and the worry it was causing both Karin and her mother. Apparently Carl had not found a buyer for something he was working on. But then, with the encouragement of Fürstenberg, he began working on a series of murals for the girls' school in Gothenburg. Urged on by Hedda Key, a teacher in the school and sister of Ellen Key, mentor to many of Karin's artist friends, Carl painted the very walls of the school—an unusual form of ornamentation for a school. He took for his subject typical figures of women in Sweden during different periods of its history—from prehistoric times to the present day of 1890. This work is somewhat ironic as it illustrated the strength and power of Sweden's women, something Carl was not one to recognize, much less celebrate.[17,18]

While Carl was away on his many trips, Karin wrote letters to him about what was going on with the family, making sure that he knew what his children were up to or letting him know that she missed him. In one letter, she wrote of being without him in Sundborn: "you have always been away when it was most beautiful. Upon your return we will make long walks together." She also wrote about Pontus, how he was "drawing on the chalkboard. Pontus got hold of the board and he did what he had seen others do, began erasing the slate, spit on it, wiped it with a cloth and looked awfully pleased." She continued in this letter, "Think I had so many little jests to tell you about the kids, but I forget."[19]

In April Carl came back home to Sundborn, evidently in good spirits. Karin wrote to her mother, telling her how much fun it was to see how happy Carl was with "us and returning home. All day he wants me to sit beside him with my work." She continued, "Dearest mother, if only I could share with you a little of my happiness." For Hilda was not happy, understandably so, as she was continuing to deal with Adolf's illness. Then on May 13, 1890, Adolf died. After a somber funeral in Hallsberg, he was buried in the Kumla graveyard, a few miles from his new Hallsberg house.[20]

Carl Larsson made a statue of the bust of the man he truly admired to be put at the gravesite. He also probably arranged for the monument that stands in the churchyard today. Hilda and Adolf never moved into the lovely home that they built, which Carl and presumably Karin helped decorate. For some time it stood empty, and then Per, Karin's younger brother, who had taken over his father's business, and his wife, Anna, and their children moved in, promptly changing the décor from the dark Nordic style to art nouveau.

On May 24, a few days after Adolf's death, Karin wrote to Carl while he was in Sandhamn, declaring how she missed her father and what a good father he had been, with his "words and deeds spread out to us children and our children." He will live in her heart, she said, and she expressed how sad her "little mother" was.[21]

Once back in Sundborn, Carl began to think about work that needed to be completed on their cottage. He worked closely with the village craftsmen, making sure that they followed his directions to the letter. For some reason he wanted an "artist's chimney," whatever that was. It seemed as if only Carl knew how it should look. But Carl could spend only so much time on the house; he needed to get back

This photograph of Carl Larsson's bust of his wife's father stands in the church yard. Photograph by Klaus Krippendorff, author's collection.

to work. Besides, the work on the cottage exhausted him, even though he tried to relax by carving furniture. While Carl had enormous strength and endurance, allowing him to party all night and then paint all day, he was getting more and more tired lately and having bouts of ill health himself.

Carl always said that when he met Karin, he was born and then was born again when he was given Adolf's cottage where he finally felt as if he were on solid ground. His rootlessness left him; he became a solid citizen, no longer a vagabond, but a farmer, a family man, and a good citizen. He longed for Karin when he was away from Sundborn, but Karin seemed more content.

It might be that her creative soul had been restored.

10

Return to Art, 1891–1893

During the winter of 1891, Carl and Karin traveled to the small village of Bingsjö, which is about 50 kilometers from Sundborn. Here Karin decided that in order to create in fabric and yarn as she wanted to, she would need to learn how to spin and weave. Spinning, the process from which fiber is converted into yarn, was done by the women of the village, who were happy to teach her this technique. Next she learned to weave, which involves working two yarns together to make a fabric. She used these processes to create various motifs on wall hangings, table runners, and rugs, depicting folk tales and legends of Sundborn.

Her work in Sundborn was often interrupted by Carl's traveling schedule and commissions. Either he left her to care for their home and children by herself, or he demanded that she travel with him, leaving the cottage and the children to the care of others. She would have been content to stay in Sundborn unhindered by his needs or demands.

Karin received a monetary inheritance from her father following his death, which she wanted to use to continue the work she and Carl had started on their little cottage after moving in. Now, with this money, she was able to do more, sooner and faster. She did not have to wait for a husband's approval, as the funds she received from her father's will allowed her to be somewhat financially independent. It did not matter whether Carl agreed with her or not; she could move ahead as she saw fit.

So, following Adolf's death, Karin and Carl both agreed that they could now build a new study, decorate the cottage's exterior, and add a porch. When they moved in, Karin had also begun work on creating a garden, but the soil was so poor that she could only create a small one at first. But even those efforts were somewhat futile. The soil only produced weeds, a few potatoes, and a lilac bush or two.[1] Now Karin also wanted to address the outside grounds in a major way.

Eventually Karin's gardens, both her vegetable and her flower gardens, would become almost as famous as her home. Karin was inspired during

104

her time in Grez to create her Sundborn gardens to produce the types of plants that she saw and enjoyed there. She also wanted her garden to maintain its "Swedishness," and planted what was commonly seen in peasant gardens. She experimented by planting seeds for plants that are not typical to Sweden: asparagus, tomatoes, spinach, and other exotic plants. She also grew narcissus, tulips, hyacinths, and lilies in pots, which she then brought into the house for decoration—a somewhat innovative decorating idea.[2]

She was aided in her gardening endeavors by her friend and neighbor, Henrika Tundal Linderdahl (1855–1931), who lived close by at Stora Hyttnäs. The two women worked in their gardens, then cooked what they had grown in their large country kitchens. They then served their creations in their dining rooms on floral tableware.[3]

According to Lena Rydin, Karin's relationship to nature was down-to-earth and practical; she had "green fingers." Karin apparently loved to dig and plant. One of the first things she planted was water lilies. Rydin explained that she and Carl took seeds and ideas home from their travels. "I have tried to plant crocuses in small cigarette boxes," she wrote to her mother.[4]

She was also one of the first, according to Rydin, to bring salad and tomatoes to the area, which she had seen grown and eaten in France. She was also able to grow azaleas and lilacs. Some of Carl's more beautiful paintings that included flower arrangements could perhaps be attributed to Karin. Through her floral compositions, she participated significantly in Carl's artwork. Although unsigned, her artistic and painterly knowledge was likely seen in these works. For example, there is one painting of Carl's where Karin is seated at a table wrapped in a plaid shawl reading a book. In it, there is a lovely flower arrangement on the table, which, according to Rydin, was probably positioned by Karin.[5]

As to the inside of the *stuga* (cottage), Karin's choice of décor was inspired by the Arts and Crafts Movement. This new way of looking at family and society as manifest in domestic arts began in England and was now gaining acceptance in Sweden. The Movement (1880–1910) emanated from the social criticism of John Ruskin (1819–1900) and the philosophy and socialist ideals of William Morris (1834–1896).

Morris, the nineteenth-century artist, printer, bookbinder, craftsman, poet, and jack-of-all-trades, advocated economic and social reform; he used design motifs from folk styles of decoration that celebrated the work of the common person. The Movement, which was a reaction against the Industrial Revolution, deemed that hand-crafted items were of better quality than those created by machines. Morris believed that rural craftspeople lived a better life than the people in cities who worked in factories, and he advocated the use of folk motifs in crafts as a way of returning to a better time. This Movement was in fact an articulation of the conflict between standardization and individuality.[6]

In England, Ruskin shared these ideas and articulated a vision of the home that became a metaphor for order in the society. The home was a place of refuge for the family, an escape from the hostile world, and its furniture and décor should reflect the individual tastes of the homeowner and homemaker—refuting the rise of industrialization.[7]

Because of this rigorous Movement, the Industrial Revolution, and the aesthetics and social principles of John Ruskin, Sweden would eventually sweep away the prevailing Victorian model of domesticity that was still in fashion and prevalent in most homes.

The Victorian era, which formally ended in 1901, placed a woman in the home, or the private space, while men occupied the public space. Motherhood and the creation of domesticity were Victorian ideals that resulted in a separation between home and work space.[8]

The home as a haven meant the creation of cozy domestic interiors, with "plush fabrics, heavy curtains and fussy furnishings which effectively cocooned the inhabitants from the world outside." There was a standard to uphold, which had implications for morality as well.[9]

In contrast the Arts and Crafts Movement, which challenged the tastes of the Victorian era, stressed individuality and argued for the notion of "fine craft." This Movement coupled good design with good society, where the worker was not brutalized by the working conditions in the factory. Ruskin thought that there should be no separation between art and society, and Morris believed that "industrialization alienated labor and created a dehumanizing distance between the designer and manufacturer. He strove to unite all the arts within the decoration of the home, emphasizing nature and simplicity of form."[10]

In the late 1890s and early 1900s, it wasn't just the Larssons who were restoring, renovating, and decorating. The rest of the world was, too, albeit in a style different from Karin's. During those years, domesticity and, by extension, the home, whether Victorian or Swedish, began to acquire a new importance. In half a century, the house was viewed as a shelter from outside forces; this was regarded as the norm. The eighteenth century had been the age of the club and the coffeehouse for those who could afford them, the gin shop and street gatherings for those who could not. Male companionship in leisure time was the norm for men. Now, especially within the class that Karin operated from—the bourgeoisie and the artist class—men and women were seen as, if not equal, at least moving toward equal footing, engaging in activities together. Certainly in Karin's world, men and women went to parties together, engaged in leisure activities like picnics and hikes, and were members of the same organizations and associations (like the Artists' Association). Women at home were looked at in a different light: they became keepers of the focus of existence (as John Ruskin was later to describe the home), the source for refuge and retreat, but also of strength and renewal.

Women like Karin did not work, so making a home was becoming a sort of art form. In lieu of gainful employment—or work as an artist, like Eva Bonnier or Julia Beck—Karin engaged in domestic arts. She was keeper of the home as housekeeper, yes, but also as designer and entrepreneur in determining almost single-handedly how the home would evolve and be decorated; Karin fully embraced this task. Her home was to be her canvas as well as a symbol of Carl's success, not just in the art world but also of his manhood.

"The British Arts and Crafts style's simplicity inspired several design movements in continental Europe: Art Nouveau in Belgium, and De Stijl in the Netherlands. The *Werkstätte* came to life in Vienna, and the *Werkbund* in Germany. Karin Larsson, along with her husband Carl Larsson, motivated Swedish design."[11]

As will be shown later, some of this philosophy is evident in the design and packaging style of IKEA, but its Swedish roots can be traced to Karin. The ideals, and especially the styles, emerging from the Arts and Crafts Movement held an immediate appeal for Karin, and she found the folklore of the Dalarna province the ideal place from which to gain inspiration and perspective on these styles in both fashion and décor. As Lena Rydin wrote, "Folk costumes were still often everyday wear. Each village had its own costume. The homes blazed with color on cupboards, walls, and doors. Textile treasures were stored in chests and lofts. Women had a strong position."[12]

Karin was likely encouraged in her efforts by two things: a changing landscape for Swedish art and crafts and the fact that her sister, Stina, was married to a British scientist, living in Wimbledon. Both Stina and her husband, Frank Bather, a British museum paleontologist, were active in the women's movement, and no doubt discussed with Karin the emerging Arts and Crafts Movement.

At the time that Karin was immersed in redoing her home, her country was establishing organizations such as the Swedish Society for Industrial Design, whose philosophy was to encourage crafts for both home and industry. The Svenska Slšjdfšreningen (Swedish Society of Craft and Industrial Design), established in 1845, fostered high standards in Swedish craft production. And the Swedish author, critic, and theorist of family life, Ellen Key (1849–1926), wrote eloquently on education and aesthetics. Her *Skönhet i hemmen* (Beauty in the home), published in *Idun* in 1897,[13] was widely read in Scandinavia and abroad. According to Barbara Miller Lane, Key argued that an aesthetic sensibility must begin in the domestic setting and beauty must be practical, useful, informed by purpose, and expressive of the soul of its user. She believed that beauty in the home was transformative—changing all of society for the better. She was influenced by the English Arts and Crafts Movement and was friends with the Larssons. She sponsored acclaimed exhibitions featuring "worker's furniture" and would also tout Karin in several years as an important influence on design.[14]

Sweden was already a leader in porcelain and glass design in Karin's day. Several design companies, like Kosta, now Kosta Boda (1742); Limmared (1741); and Orreforsks (1898), operated out of southern Sweden. They were all known for lyrical decoration on light and simple glass forms. The art of glassmaking came to Sweden in the 1500s, arriving from Germany and Italy. Because of Sweden's geography of large forests, ample supply of sand, and other raw materials, glassmakers could operate all over the country. Ironically it was industrialization that brought glass into the reach of most people. With the production of so much glass and porcelain, Sweden became a leader in creation and sales, but it was not until 1825 that Swedish glass finally gained international recognition for its quality, beauty, and craftsmanship.[15]

Sweden was also becoming known for establishing museums that preserved the country's national heritage, such as the great outdoor museum, Skansen, founded in Stockholm in 1891. This amazing enterprise celebrated rural Swedish life, of which Sundborn was a perfect example. The museum exhibited then and now furnished houses and farmsteads, cultivated plots, and gardens that illustrate different social conditions throughout the centuries.[16]

All of this was going on in Sweden—and Europe—at the same time that Karin was emerging from her artistic cocoon, that self-imposed (or Carl-imposed) isolation from art making. Her artistry had lain fallow for about six or seven years, but when she found herself with a home of her own in a village she was familiar with from having spent time there with her grandparents as a child, her artistic side was reawakened. Now she could be an artist in a way that would not compete with her dominant husband and would allow her to continue mentoring him and caring for her children. Textiles and domestic art became her métier.

As Lena Rydin explains, "She made textiles for the home, created her own fashion for herself and the children, designed furniture and lent a joyful atmosphere to everyday family life. As can be seen in Carl's paintings, she arranged beautiful and original still-lifes of flowers. Everything she did expressed a new way of thinking. She made the little village in Dalarna into her vantage point on the world."[17]

Color was a dominant theme in Dalarna—and Sundborn—and Karin's use of color from her painting days resurfaced in Sundborn in her needlework. All through the 1890s, Karin worked on her weaving and textile artistry, becoming more and more proficient all the time. She would weave stories into her work, stories through motifs such as a family tree. Her work also had elements of Japanese and modern art, although Carl was no proponent of the latter. She was able to mix patterns and colors into a decorative whole.

Karin was especially taken by the work of Kate Greenaway (1846–1901), an English children's book illustrator and writer. Greenaway's illustrations of children, especially of the clothing they wore, were embraced by those who were philosophically inclined toward the Arts and Crafts Movement. Ruskin and Greenaway had a friendship that was initiated when Ruskin wrote Greenaway a letter of admiration in 1880. Their relationship, mostly through letters (some 500 sent by Ruskin, more by Greenaway), lasted until his death. Their styles and ideals influenced each other through their correspondence.[18]

Greenaway dressed the young children in her stories in her own version of late eighteenth-century and Regency fashion: smocked frocks, pinafores, high-waisted dresses, and straw bonnets. A full generation of mothers in the liberal-minded, "artistic" British circles of the 1880s and 1890s imitated the style, dressing their daughters in Kate Greenaway pantaloons and bonnets. Karin read Greenaway's *Under the Window* in its Swedish translation, *Smått Folk* (Little People). Karin's sister, Stina, corresponded frequently with Karin about decorating her home in Kensington in a style of the "English aesthetes."[19]

Karin herself adored this style and began creating her own version of the "Greenaway fashion," mingling local Dalarna folk features with Greenaway style into the clothing designs she sewed for herself and for her children. She began to wear loose-fitting gowns covered with patterned aprons and often wore a wide-brimmed Greenaway straw bonnet, perhaps given to her by her Aunt Elsie. The clothing she made for herself allowed for great movement, such as bending over in the garden or getting down on one's hands and knees to refurbish furniture. Her designs were colorful and usually covered in a wide decorative, but serviceable, apron. She was also uncorseted, rejecting yet another Victorian custom for women.

For her children she made pinafores similar to those worn by the women who worked in Sundborn. Karin employed many Sundborn women to cook, watch the children, clean, and garden. She did these things herself,

This is one of Kate Greenaway's sketches, titled "Polly," a character from *The Queen of the Pirate Isle*, by Bret Harte, illustrated by Kate Greenaway (1885). The outfit that the child is wearing, loose-fitted dress with an over-apron, will be recreated by Karin for her and her daughters' use. Project Gutenberg eText.

too, but, as a woman from the upper classes, she was used to servants and used them wisely so that she could concentrate on her art making and renovating her home.

Karin also reverted to *Japonisme*, which she used in her fabric making and other decorative creations. She had investigated this style of painting while working in Grez. The style is specific to the French and mainly found expression in Impressionism, while in England it initially influenced the decorative arts. Artists were especially influenced by its lack of perspective and shadow, with flat areas of strong color and the compositional freedom gained by placing the subject off center, mostly with a low diagonal axis to the background. This type of art can be seen in Carl's work, where he places the dominant figure, usually Karin, in an off-centered position.[20]

In 1891 a major exhibition was launched at the Royal Garden in Stockholm of the style created by Gustav III, who ascended the throne after returning to Sweden from an extended stay at the court of Louis VI at Versailles. It can be assumed that both Karin and Carl attended the exhibition, as it seemed to be another source of inspiration for Karin. This Gustavian style, as reinterpreted by the Swedes and particularly by Karin, was not of the regal gilded Francophile ornamentation but a scaled down "countrified look." The Gustavian tenets of light, refinement, and unpretentious elegance are evident in the rooms of the Sundborn cottage. Michael Snodin describes the overall effect of the Larsson cottage with its various styles comingled into what is now called Modern Swedish Design as a retreat from urbanism and a "distillation of Swedishness in line with the national romantic movement and the linked drive to preserve a rapidly disappearing folk culture."[21]

Karin was very happy in Sundborn and would have been content to spend most of her time there. However, in January of 1891, Carl sent an imploring letter to her almost demanding that she bring herself and the children to Stockholm, which she did. The family returned to the capital where Karin, her three children, and Hilda were once again living in the small flat on Linnegatan—while Carl went on to Gothenburg. There Karin found herself pregnant with her fourth child.[22]

While living in Stockholm, Karin wrote to Carl in Gothenburg, continuing once again to express some of her frustration at the many separations, saying, "Thus you shall know that I have not much more than four weeks left [until the birth of her child].… Every night I dream that you intend to get engaged and remarry, and that does not put me in such a good mood during the day."[23]

And then on February 18, Karin delivered another girl, Lisbeth. It is unclear whether Carl made it back to Stockholm for the birth, but what Karin's Swedish biographer does suggest is that Karin had misgivings about Carl remaining in Gothenburg and working at Valand, the art school. He encouraged them to come to him. Following Lisbeth's birth, Karin left the boys with her mother and went to meet Carl with Suzanne to help with the baby, where they lived in a house provided by Fürstenberg—his summer cottage. Karin made the home livable for her and the children, and then she returned to retrieve her other children from Stockholm.[24]

While in Gothenburg, Carl became ill. He had chronic troubles with his stomach. His physicians prescribed medication and diet, and he was told that he should not be going to so many parties. Nonetheless he continued to attend various events and celebrations held by his numerous acquaintances, leaving Karin home alone with the children.

Apparently their stay in Gothenburg was not to Karin's liking. She wrote in her *dagbok* (diary): "Today I have been furious with Carl. He has been a long time eating dinner at the Fürstenbergs where he enjoys their party. Today, he should just be at home as I had made mutton with *pomme frite*, really French. I see that he will not be here today, either. Not only the wasted dinner but I was alone. I am a martyr."[25]

Karin at least found the time to work on her textile designs, however, and her thoughts were never far from the pleasures of life at the cottage. For the Sundborn dining table, she envisioned a white lace cloth embroidered with a wildflower motif and began working on it. While in Stockholm during that winter, she thought about the daisies and bluebells she would handpick and place in a large glass jar which she would set in the center of the table. She planned outdoor dining under the sheltering leaves and branches of the huge birch. The birds would hum or squawk, depending upon their nature, the bees buzz, the flowers blossom, and the air would be pungent both day and night.

Soon they were back in Sundborn for the summer. Carl was still not well and was sleeping a great deal, but Karin felt great being back in her cottage. Carl's anger at being ignored by the artistic community was ever-present, even though he was winning prizes and commissions. It was Carl's nature to be frustrated easily by what he thought of as rebuffs of his many proposals for the fresco for the Nationalmuseum. During this time he was still working on other suggested commissions and was being paid by Fürstenberg.

In Sundborn and also when the family was back in Stockholm, Carl continued to pursue a heavy-handed painting style. He was determined to create a genuinely Swedish art form. He still preferred oils, even though he had had some success in Grez using watercolors at Karin's suggestion.[26]

It would not be until the summer of 1894 back in Sundborn, at the behest of his wife, that Carl—with two more children in the Larsson household (Brita born in 1893 and Mats in 1894)—would begin painting the water-colors that would make him famous and rich and his family known all over Europe.

Eventually Karin, too, would get her chance to shine—with a light that would not dim. Until then she made her peace with the loss of painting and used her creativity in raising children, designing family clothing, coun-seling her husband, entertaining, and—most importantly—renovating Lilla Hyttnäs.

11

The Swedish Room, 1894

In the spring of 1893, Carl and Karin were still in Gothenburg, where Carl was getting ready to hand over the post of head of Valand to his old friend, Georg Pauli, which he did in April. Then Carl and Karin temporarily moved to a fisherman's cottage in Marstrand, a small seaside community near Gothenburg on the west coast of Sweden. Carl was sleeping poorly but still continued to paint, asking Karin and the children to pose for his newest endeavor: *De Mina*, a collection of paintings about his "dear ones." Karin was pregnant with their fifth child, Brita, who was born on May 10, 1893. While Karin was giving birth in a shack, Carl continued painting.[1]

According to Carl's recollection, the *mina* (poor thing), as he called Karin, crept into the corner of the sofa awaiting the birth. The new baby smiled at two weeks, so Carl reported, but Karin looked dark and depressed.[2] To commemorate Brita's birth, Carl created a watercolor, *Karin, Brita at the Breast*. One can only wonder how Karin felt about delivering a child in a seaside fisherman's shack and then having to model with the new child for her husband.[3]

In a letter to Fürstenberg, Carl wrote: "Here is the most beautiful place on earth, that's for sure. Everything is in the springtime and a better time to have a child cannot be imagined."[4]

Finally the family returned to Sundborn on the first of June of the same year. Upon their return the village population greeted them with waving and cheering, and in their yards the Swedish flag was hoisted. Carl was in a good mood, sleeping well, and feeling healthy, but Karin, now with four children and a newborn baby, must have been busy, although daughter Suzanne was a big help to her mother.[5]

While they enjoyed the summer in Sundborn, they were soon back on the road. Carl was once again in Stockholm working in Georg Pauli's studio (while Pauli was taking on Carl's duties in Gothenburg). The family lived on Glasbrnksgatan 15 in a rented flat with two studios. Carl was still trying to get his proposal commissioned for the murals decorating the lower

113

stairwell at the Nationalmuseum, which the government finally approved on February 2, 1894. To prepare for this monumental work, Carl and Karin traveled throughout Europe, leaving the children with Hilda, as Carl wanted to visit various museums to study frescos. Karin wrote to her mother in April 1894, "On the road between Lund and Malmö [Sweden], beloved mother and the little ones … a thousand kisses that you can share with the little ones."[6]

The couple traveled through Germany, then Italy to Assisi and Perugia, and then Rome—even though Karin was pregnant again with their sixth child. Finally they returned to Paris, where Carl studied fresco techniques. Karin seemed happy to be spending time with Carl. They visited churches and little villages and did a lot of walking. Karin wrote to her mother, "I feel very good. Carl claims that I look like a flower."[7]

They returned to Stockholm in early summer after four months of travel, where they picked up their children and returned to Sundborn.

During the summer of 1894, it seemed as if the rain would never stop. It was the summer in which the Larsson family had decided to live in Sundborn full-time, giving up their residences in Stockholm and Gothenburg.

What is usually a glorious season in Sweden was ushered in by a different kind of weather this year. Instead of the typical brilliant, sun-filled days, this summer it was rain, rain, and more rain. Karin—along with Carl, the children, and their dog—traveled by train from Stockholm to Falun Centralstation. They took a carriage from the station to the cottage they had been restoring, which they decided was at last ready for them to live in year-round. Often frail and suffering in the Stockholm winters from pneumonia and other respiratory illnesses, Karin felt rejuvenated by moving permanently to Sundborn, even though by the summer she was quite large with her latest pregnancy.

In Sweden, summer light almost never ends, and it was usually a delight for the children to play outside while the adults savored the joy of living in the fresh air after months inside during Sweden's glistening and brutal winter. Days in *Midsommer*—June and July—can be 22 hours long. The summer light extended Carl's painting day and allowed Karin, a dedicated gardener, special time in the yard. She would be out early in the morning in one of her handmade lavender flowing frocks with the white apron and the wide-brimmed straw bonnet, and would stay late into the evening tending to the flower beds, weeding out dandelions from the green lawn, and fertilizing her vegetable garden, which was now producing food for the table. In summers past when the family came to Sundborn for a few weeks, family meals were always taken outside overlooking the creek, especially at festival time or when the family entertained guests.

The outdoor dining table would be covered in a white lace cloth, embroidered by Karin with a wildflower motif. And, as in her Stockholm imaginings, Karin would handpick daisies and bluebells and place them in a large glass jar set in the center of the table, which was under the sheltering leaves and branches of the huge birch.

This summer, however, was the Larsson family's summer of discontent.

While it was warm, it continued to rain without letting up. The always positive Karin wondered how to keep seven children occupied (and a restless and grumpy husband calm). Everyone was edgy as the unusual and intolerable rain continued for six straight weeks. Karin, normally happily busy and temperate, was even getting a little frustrated, not only because of the weather and the enforced confinement, but also with Carl. He returned to his often irritable and unhappy state. Carl, whose murals at the time covered Sweden's public buildings and museums, confessed in his memoir that he "went about in an insufferable mood."[8]

Carl could be depressed and neurotic in general, but with the added factor of being shut up in the house all day, he was becoming particularly difficult. He clung to his wife's skirts like a whiney child, asking her to look at his latest painting, or to come to the studio, or to sit in the library and read reviews of his work.

But Karin had her own revived creative endeavors, which had been cut short by Carl's disdain for female artists. For the first 10 years of their marriage, she had been content to be that woman behind the genius. She knew firsthand that if you scratch an artist you would find a muse (or two) somewhere just out of the reach, in the shadows. For most of these artists, the muse would act as nurse, mistress, nanny, and bodyguard, standing famously and perpetually on watch. Sometimes the woman defied convention and publicly flourished herself. Others, like Camille Claudel, the sculptress, who was a student at the Académie Colarossi during the time Karin was in Paris, came to a bad end. She was Auguste Rodin's muse and model, as well as his lover. No doubt Karin followed their saga, played out across Paris, which ended with Claudel eventually being committed to an asylum. She was both talented, perhaps a genius herself, and disturbed.

Karin also watched her friend, Eva Bonnier, a student in the women's section with her at the Royal Swedish Academy of Fine Arts. Eva, whose best years as an artist and portraitist were in Paris between the years 1883–1890, was awarded a number of honors such as *mention honorable* at the Salon de Paris and recognition at the 1893 World's Fair.[9] She never married, suffered from depressions, and died after falling from a window at the Hotel Cosmopolitan on January 13, 1909, in Copenhagen.[10] Karin, who saw these and many other examples of women's struggles, "made the strategic choice as a woman, and later found an artistic area in which she would not be in competition with Carl."[11]

Like other less flamboyant women who continued to pursue their own art, often in obscurity and certainly in their own way, Karin was in the process of returning to her creative enterprises while living a domesticated and simple life. And so during this dingy June, Karin was trying to finish both her bedroom, which she shared with the children, and Carl's bedroom, which he slept in alone. Both rooms had been newly constructed during the last year and now Karin wanted to create bedcovers, curtains, and other tapestries.

While immersed in her own work, Karin also had to put up with Carl. She was annoyed at her husband for following her around like one of the toddlers, impatiently demanding attention. She finally begged him to do something, anything, to escape what could devolve into one of his depressions.

She might have said something like, "Go sketch something." It would not have been said in exasperation, for she rarely gave in to such behavior. Eventually he did retrieve his paints from his studio in an attempt to both keep Karin happy, which he loved to do, and improve his own mood.

During that summer of the unusual rain, Karin was almost 35 years old and perhaps at the height of her beauty, and most certainly at the apex of her creativity and artistry. Made iconic in portraits created by her husband, Karin is thin with dark hair and eyes, agile, and tall. Carl's sketches and watercolors wrap her in the mysterious aura of the beloved woman. She is often turned away from him, shown in profile, or hidden from view by a large sun hat. Sometimes blooming flowers hide her face and, in many ways, her identity.

It has been written about her that "she was portrayed as the male fantasy of the idealized, undemanding woman, made to be worshipped without giving anything in return."[12] She was Carl's perpetual subject, of great importance to him, and he loved her deeply. But he never seemed to view her as others did—hard-working, humorous, down-to-earth; she was a woman capable of entertaining Sweden's illustrious artistic community while managing a large, expanding family, and renovating, one room at a time, a disreputable cottage.

In fact, the real Karin was less distant and perhaps more defiant than ever acknowledged. In photographs she faces the camera, if not the easel, and even smiles. Her face is wide and she still has those strong, dark eyebrows of her youth—almost reaching across her forehead—and her hair is parted in the middle. She is uncorseted (unusual in those days) and wears long, brilliantly colored gowns that drape, swoop, and flow—gowns she designed herself. She often appears serious, and this was especially true as a young girl, the 14- or 18-year-old Karin. Yet she was mostly happy and seemingly content with her life, and always busy.

Now in this summer of rain, she was forced to give Carl something to do because he was restless and unbearable. As he painted his watercolors beside her, he was ready to paint yet another picture of her. Karin, perhaps now getting a little testy, may have said that she was too busy to be a model for him right then. But he wanted her to tell him what his next job would be. He also wanted her to know that she was important to him and that he could not do his work without her.

Karin thought it would be a good idea if Carl were to immortalize their dear little cottage by painting the rooms, with family in them, as each room was finished. About this idea Carl wrote, "I decided to get busy at what I had been dreaming of for a long time—to draw souvenir pictures from my little home. I thought it would be a kind of family document. (Well, it was really Karin's idea: with a view to giving me something to do.)"[13]

The newly finished drawing room, which would eventually be called "the Swedish room" and known all over the world, was Karin's special joy, her most innovative creation. It was the first room of the cottage finished to her satisfaction.The family loved this room. Carl called it a "temple of idleness." It was indeed the picture of comfort and peace: with the family dog, Kapo, sleeping on the woven throw rug, the inviting couch with loose blue pillows and blankets, the knitting and needlework spilling out onto the floor, the chess and checkerboard ready for a match, and playing cards. Karin was proud of the room, and to signify that she was finished with it— that her artistic work was done for that room, at least—she suggested to Carl that he paint it. Carl, following his wife's injunction as he had done many times before, spent many days during that rainy season capturing its beauty and serenity.

Eventually Carl painted a number of versions of the drawing room. One called *Put in the Punishment Corner* shows their six-year-old son, Pontus, being banished to the blue-and-white room for some infraction or another. Other sketches, *Flowers on the Windowsill* and *The Relaxing Corner*, depict light flooding into the plant-filled room, pushing its way past the glass of the vertical windows. That set of windows, overlooking the rippling Sundborn creek where soon the rain would stop and the children would catch crayfish, brought nature into the room.

Karin arranged this drawing room like a Gustavian stateroom: she placed chairs along the walls and constructed a raised dais with a white

This painting completed by Carl, *The Cosy Corner*, is an example of Karin's new style. Nationalmuseum (Stockholm)/Wikimedia Sverige.

railing, creating a room within a room. This gave the impression of space, despite being filled with furniture. Bright and informal—with wood paneling, simple white furniture, plain pine floors, and checkered fabrics—the ambiance is the epitome of Swedish interior design.

A summer atmosphere pervaded the room, even in the deepest and darkest days of the Swedish winter. It was in this room that Karin most effectively captured the eighteenth-century countrified atmosphere and updated it for her own time. This Gustavian style was purposively chosen by Karin as it was the type of décor found in small manor houses and country homes. It was not the Louis XVI silk and gilt style for upper-middle class families, nor was it the Victorian splendor of velvet and dark wood.

Karin had begun her renovations by using furniture already in the house when her two aunts lived there, but she updated it with paint, fabric, and color. She displayed undraped windows, refinished the furniture and painted it white, upholstered her sofas and chairs in her famous blue-and-white style, and painted the walls bright colors. Children played in this drawing room—unlike in Victorian homes. They ran in and out and rummaged through their mother's many sewing baskets to look for materials

This image of the dining room shows the family getting ready to play the Swedish card game, *Vira*. Nationalmuseum (Stockholm)/Wikimedia Sverige.

to fashion costumes for holiday and festival plays. Also atypical for that time, this drawing room parlor was not formal. Karin refused to follow the custom of hanging paintings of dead ancestors in ornate frames.

At this time, they entertained frequently in Sundborn. Carl used to invite the villagers into the drawing room to play the card game, *Vira*. And Karin would host some of Sweden's most famous people, such as Selma Lagerlöf, the first woman to receive the Nobel Prize in Literature.

Advances in technology, improved sanitation and hygiene, the emergence of an increasingly affluent middle class, and the movement of work from the home to the office and the factory separated wives from their husbands. As stated earlier, the women therefore became solely housewives and also became increasingly interested in the decorative arts. The home developed into a symbol of the success of the breadwinner and an illustration of the respectability of the family. In the Victorian style, public rooms meant that homes were on display and, thus, how they were received by the world was more important than the comfort and convenience of the family.

Drawing rooms, parlors, halls, dining rooms, and morning rooms were tended to by the housewife-decorator (more than bedrooms, bathrooms, kitchens, and nurseries) as they were on display for the "public." Because of the rigorous Arts and Crafts Movement, the Industrial Revolution, and the aesthetic and social principles of John Ruskin, Sweden would eventually sweep away the Victorian model of domesticity.

But that would come later.

Now Karin's ideas were something unusual. The freedom of her designs would at some point be the envy of those living with dark, somber Victorian pretentiousness. Those dark Victorian rooms, filled with heavy furniture, dark velvet drapes, and unused front rooms would soon be replaced by her textiles: wall hangings, bed coverings, tablecloths, and pillow covers.

One of her projects, a table cover embroidered in a lattice stitch and made with red cotton, illustrated a tree of life pattern, symbolizing the Larsson family. It has been written that "the portière the 'Rose of Love' between the couple's separate bedrooms was one of Karin Larsson's boldest, freest and most time-consuming textile enterprises. The challenge was to weave a curtain, which would not reduce the light in the inner, darker room. Karin's solution was a tapestry with a loose warp." The simple motif is surrounded by macramé in many interlacing patterns.[14]

Another tapestry, created in 1903, *Four Elements*, was made to fit over a sofa in the dining room. The colors were vibrant and illustrated earth, water, air, and fire—all shown in abstract patterns. The center motif was both a cross and a maypole.[15] Then there is Karin's *Sunflower*, which dates from 1905, and is frequently copied. It was sewn on a blue background, using green, yellow, and brownish black silk floss. Sunflowers were one of the favorite motifs of the Aesthetic Movement, which both Larssons followed, but Karin's free treatment of the flower was creative and uniquely hers.[16]

So while the rain poured down on Sundborn, Karin worked and, in response to Carl's paralysis, demanded that he paint her emerging creations—which he did, even though he balked.

Maybe Karin suggested that she would set him up herself in the drawing room. To do so she would have had to drop her own work to prop him up both emotionally and physically—as usual.

He may have said, in a petulant voice: "Why would I want to paint a room?"

And no doubt she had to tell him because he couldn't paint anything else in the pouring rain. And she probably suggested that he use watercolors.

While Carl preferred to work in oils, Karin more or less insisted that he work in watercolors and that he shrink his vision from mural-size to room-size. And so, because of the rain and because he had nothing better to do, he began to paint—and he eventually created at least 20 watercolors of Karin's blue-and-white room. After a few versions of just the room, Karin asked him to add the children. And so he put in his children in various poses: on the couch reading, petting the dog, playing chess.

That summer of discontent ended with Carl creating lovely watercolors of their home that would become beloved and imitated all over Europe. And Karin, too, engaged in an additional creative endeavor, bearing another son, Mats, who came into the world in Sundborn on November 24, 1894.

A few years after that summer, Carl exhibited the watercolors of his home at the 1897 World Exhibition in Stockholm. These charming scenes of bucolic domesticity immediately captivated audiences. Thus, the rooms of the lovely little cottage came to the attention of Swedes and others around Europe from reports of the exhibition and because of the many publications of the watercolors which sprang from it.

So lovely were these watercolors from that rainy summer that Carl published 24 of them (pictures not only of the drawing room, but of the garden and other rooms in the house) following his success at the exhibition in a series called *Ett hem* (At home) (1899). Because of the success of this book, Karin urged him to paint more in order to create another book. And hence a new so-called art form was born.

12

The Innovator, 1895–1904

The year 1895 began poorly for Karin.

Baby Mats, born in November, was weak from birth and did not seem to thrive. The family left their home in Sundborn and returned to Stockholm for the New Year, where Mats took a turn for the worse and died on January 19, 1895. Karin wrote to her mother, "Little mother! Our little boy fell asleep then died slowly this morning. He has already been wrapped in white. We are grateful that we had him as long as we did."[1]

Karin had to bear this loss alone as Carl was not with her very much that year. He was kept out of the house with his responsibilities with both the Statens Inköpsnämnd (National Purchasing Committee), where he was responsible for purchasing art works, and as Chairman of the Konstnärsklubben (Artists' Club). He was also busy making what he called "cartoons" for the Nationalmusueum frescos. He even traveled to Gothenburg with his friend, Georg Pauli, to study the frescoes there.

Karin was pregnant again by June, with the family staying in Sundborn for the summer. They returned to Stockholm in the fall and then, at the end of the year, returned to Sundborn for Christmas. Kersti was born on March 31, 1896—another little girl for the family.

Perhaps the birth of two children in quick succession and the death of Mats were too much for Karin. Although at times she had serious bouts of respiratory infections, she was generally infrequently ill. But at the beginning of 1897, in the cold and sleet from January until April, Karin lay abed seriously ill with pneumonia. Carl wrote: "A couple of times I was close to losing my wife to pneumonia. That gave me a lot to think about, for what would my life be without her."[2]

Many thought that without Karin, Carl would not have reached the heights that he did. His own personality was so at odds with success—his depressions, paranoid personality, angry outbursts, and his, some might call, psychosomatic illnesses such as migraine headaches, sleeping difficulties, and stomach problems. Karin was always there to support him and encourage him.

122

Their Sundborn housekeeper, Martina Eriksson, recounted how once Carl was finished working on a painting, he would call Karin into the studio to see what else needed to be done with it. According to Martina they would stand there together, arms around each other, Karin looking at the work and Carl waiting for her assessment. Martina saw this finishing of Carl's work, this discussion about lines and colors, as a ritual of sorts, but which Martina said she herself did not understand. She recalled that they would continue to look at the work and then Karin would say, "Carl, it's fine."[3]

In any event, Carl was lost without Karin, and her recovery this year was slow. Her fever would abate and then return. She would get up and then have a relapse and have to return to bed. The village physician, Sam Hall, practically set up home in Karin's bed chamber. Dr. Carlsson from Falun was called in. A nurse stayed with her. Even the self-sacrificing midwife called on her.[4]

Carl was busy in Stockholm working on the decorations for the newly built Opera House, which consisted of gold stuccos and ceiling paintings in the Golden Foyer, when he received a call from a physician requesting he contact Karin's mother—Karin was that ill. Karin stayed at Lilla Hytttnäs during her illness, while Hilda took care of the rest of the family in Hallsberg—the children, Ulf, Pontus, Lisbeth, and the new baby, Kersti, who was about six months old and had just sprouted her first teeth.[5] Suzanne at 13 stayed behind with her mother to take on the duties of housekeeper and keep watch over her.

The thought of losing his wife—always strong and courageous—was inconceivable to Carl. Seeing her ill made him even more anxious than normal. While he was still in Stockholm in mid–January, he received another call: Karin was worse. She was spitting up blood and the fever had returned in full force. A consulting physician was called in. Telephone calls and telegrams went back and forth from Sundborn to Stockholm—and to Hallsberg. Should Carl come or stay? Back and forth he paced, not knowing what to do, waiting for yet another telegram. He spent that night in a lather, awaiting the bad news from Dr. Carlsson that Karin had declined even further. As he stood on the train platform ready to return to Sundborn, minutes before boarding the train Carl received the telegram saying she was all right.[6]

The good doctor had cured her "with a capsule to the lung" and calmed everyone down in the process.[7]

Finally Carl heard from Karin herself: "Loved! Loved! I just enjoy, enjoy coming back to life."[8] A note was sent to Hilda in Hallsberg to let her know that finally all was well.

After she had recovered from that first bout of illness, Karin returned to their flat in Stockholm, ready to take up her duties: raising children, keeping house, entertaining guests, and being there for Carl as his muse and model. But once there she succumbed again.

Carl painted a lovely watercolor of Karin in bed during this illness, this time from influenza, which he titled *Convalescence* (1899). The painting tells the story of one of her illnesses: pink on the walls and floor, pink flowers on the bed stand, giving the room a soft comforting glow, while Karin, rarely shown not working or engaged in some task, lies silent. She looks wan and is facing toward the painter with a pink shawl draped over her shoulder, contrasting with her thin, white face. This is a unique portrait, as Carl generally posed Karin either with her back to the viewer or half-eclipsed by hats with netting or blooms or turned sideways. Rarely is she facing front.

Perhaps this was Carl's way of expressing his fear of her dying—if he could have her facing him as he painted, not hidden, not engaged, but there looking at him and for him, he could be reassured that she would always

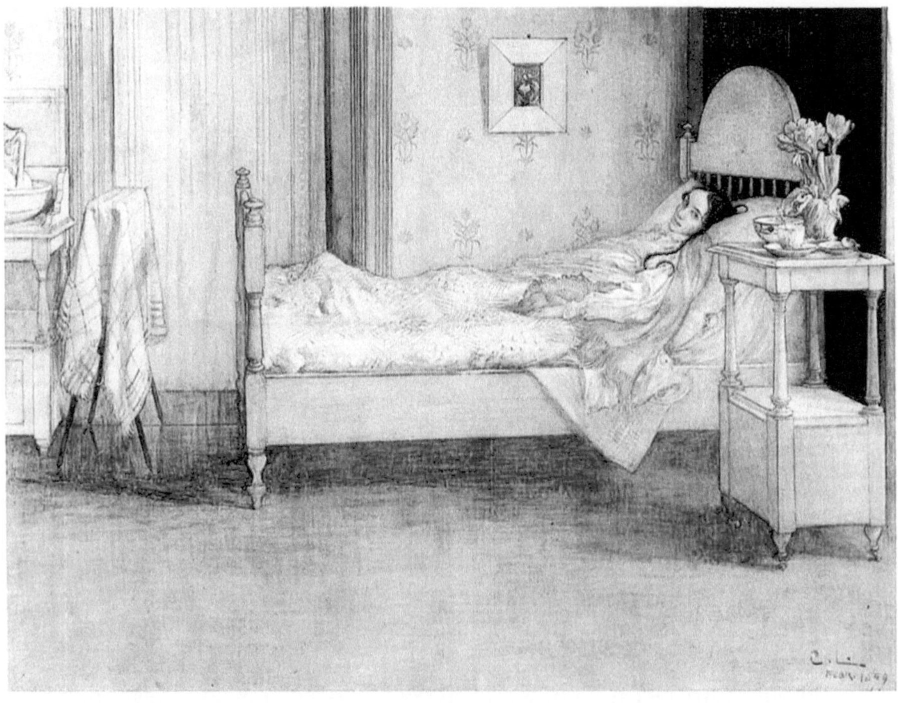

This image is of Karin abed, with influenza. She was frequently ill when living in Stockholm. Carl called this *Convalescence* (1899). Nationalmuseum (Stockholm)/Wikimedia Sverige.

be there to encourage, placate, and please him. Soon thereafter in April, Karin returned to Sundborn from Stockholm. And so the year went, with Karin ill off and on, the children with their grandmother off and on, Carl in Stockholm, coming back and forth to Sundborn, and then finally Karin well enough to be with the family—debilitated, but slowly recovering.

While in Sundborn Carl was his usual restless self and went back and forth to Stockholm to continue working on the Opera House, which was finished in December 1897. In the meantime, he continued using watercolors to paint scenes of domesticity—scenes from his own family life.

It had become fashionable for middle-class Swedish families to have their homes photographed, showing off their rooms and the family members who peopled them. They would then put these photos into "elegantly bound albums, as a history of the home and family so that the families' domestic life could be admired by others."[9]

Carl's unique contribution to this pastime—at Karin's behest, of course—was to create a series of short, funny tales and pictures of family life, especially of the children, which he completed following that rainy summer of 1894. The sketches, done in black and white, were published by the Albert Bonniers publishing house in a volume called *De mina* (My loved ones) (1895). This would not be the most successful of Carl's publishing ventures—his *Ett hem*, mentioned earlier, was the most successful—but these sketches portraying the Larsson family at home would be a foreshadowing of what was to come from future publishing ventures.[10]

Carl and Karin were known socially to Karl Otto Bonnier (1856–1941), of the famous Bonnier publishing dynasty, and his sister, Eva, was Karin's dear friend (and, as noted earlier, the fiercest critic of her decision to give up her art).

Bonnier went to see the *Ett hem* exhibition in Dalarna; subsequently, the famous publishing house obtained the rights to the paintings. Karl Otto wanted to publish a monograph and asked Carl to write the text for the paintings. Ann J. Topjon, Professor Emeritus, Whittier College, wrote, "In this work, Larsson extolled the virtues of his home, and unpretentiously held it up as a design model for others to follow, a drastic change from the dark Victorian interiors then prevalent. The innovations and creativity found in his home, produced in large part by Karin, started a revolution in interior decoration that has continued even today."[11]

The book, *Ett hem*, was published two years later in December 1899 and became one of the most successful of all of Bonnier's publications. It also marked the beginning of the fame Carl and his family would achieve all over Sweden and eventually all over northern Europe. Among its 26 watercolors, various rooms in the home were highlighted, such as the blue-

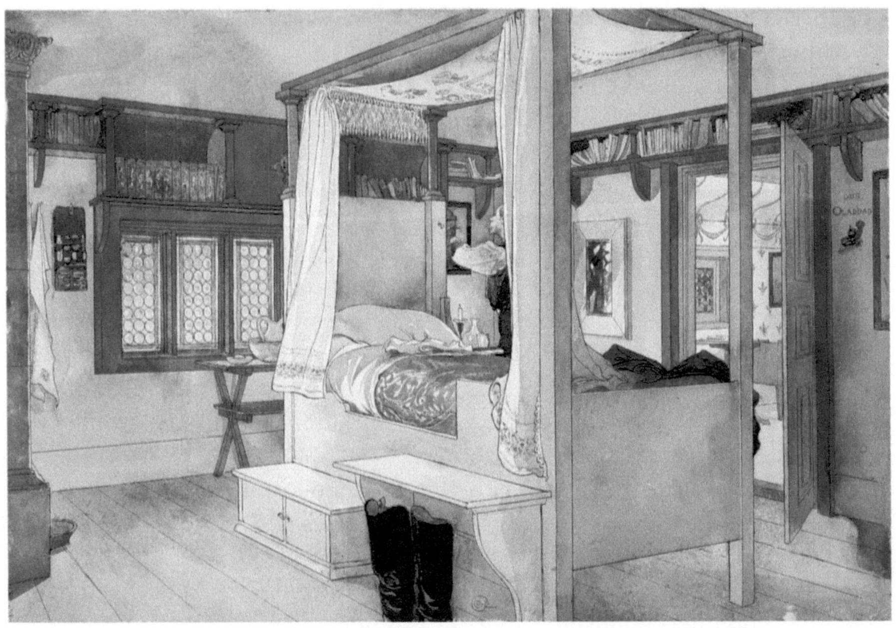

This image shows Carl's bedroom, where he slept alone. All the fabric was created and decorated by Karin. Nationalmuseum (Stockholm)/Wikimedia Sverige.

and-white Gustavian drawing room, which has been described as providing the visitor with a deep sense of comfort. Even in winter the room had a sense of summer, with its plants, white table, and undraped windows with a view over Sundborn creek.[12]

Carl's red-and-white room is shown with his bed in the center—he felt this produced better and deeper sleep. The walls are whitewash, the trim red. The bed is draped in white flowing curtains with a red embroidered border. The coverlet of the bed is also red with a floral design, and was both designed and woven by Karin.

The family dining room is also predominantly red—red-painted table, chairs, bench, and window trim—and features green paneling, which gives it a bright and happy impression. This was a room that the Larssons used all the time, where they introduced to Sundborn and to the rest of Sweden the French habit of remaining a long time at the dining table for conversation. Karin's woven tapestry, *The Four Elements*, is shown hanging over the dining room bench. Once again, plants and flowers abound; the wide-plank, wooden floors are not covered by rugs. By the way, the adults did not eat separately, but with the children who were free to roam around the home. No space, not even Carl's studio, was forbidden to them.[13]

Images from the family's life outdoors are also depicted by Carl's watercolors. The family loved having breakfast under the birch tree. There are scenes of naked children diving off the board into the creek and paintings of the outside of the house with trees and flowers, which were important to both Karin and Carl.

There is a relaxed and homey ambiance shown in these watercolors, yet a richness in the color and the fabrics. This is a lovely and elegant home, as painted by Carl, and yet one that is not the least bit Victorian and stuffy. It is a home where children and friends feel comfortable, without the heavy atmosphere so prevalent in those days—no velvet drapes on windows, antimacassars on the backs of sofas and chairs, or heavy dark furniture, and no sunless rooms.

Ett hem was to be a manifesto for a new ideal of life and living. The paintings were done in large form so that the details of the rooms were shown clearly to the readers who had never experienced home décor that was both charming and innovative, given that both Sweden and Germany were following the prevailing style set by the Victorians.

And then in the midst of all these publications and fame, to ring in the new century Karin delivered yet another child—her eighth. Little Esbjörn was born in May 1900, somewhat of a surprise to Karin and the other children. Kersti was only four at the time, but pictures of the little toddler fascinated the reading public, who were entranced with the beautiful Karin, her lovely clothing, and her adorable children.

Everything was exciting and new, and fame, along with the financial security it provided, made the family ecstatic.

There were multiple publications following this initial one—seven by 1920, the year after Carl's death—all created with Karin's encouragement and support. Carl came to be one of the most prolific book illustrators in Sweden, surpassing famous authors such as August Strindberg, Selma Lagerlöf, and others, and Carl worked closely with Bonniers for years. Karl-Otto became somewhat of a mentor to Carl.

There was little interest in Carl's *Ett hem* initially, except in Sweden. Soon, however, Bonnier was able to persuade a German publisher to take a look at the book, as Nordic writers were popular in Germany. "The result was an inexpensive book in a reduced format with 16 color reproductions. By heavily cutting and pasting Jungbeck-Grønland's translation, Langewiesche produced a Larsson book which would appeal to the Germans. The art's interior design ideas gave way to an idyllic almost religious image of a happy, sunny home centered on children."[14]

Carl's second publication, a sequel of sorts to *Ett hem* entitled *Larssons*, was published at Christmastime in 1902. The focus of this book was on family life rather than on individual rooms in the Sundborn cottage, as was depicted in *Ett hem*. This second book, *Larssons*, also made its entrance beyond Sweden with publication in Germany and showcased Carl's children and home. Here the little girls are shown wearing dresses that Karin designed and sewed—pinafores with aprons, and fabric bonnets, just like those depicted in the Kate Greenaway books. There are paintings of celebrations in Carl's studio where a long table covered with a white lace cloth was brought in and filled to overflowing with all kinds of food and drink. Around the table children in gaily colored dresses get ready to dine; the maid carries food to the table, and Carl sits in a chair speaking with family members. The scenes totally captivated the book's readers. Everyone wanted to wear Karin's clothing, dress their children as she did, and live as they did in these beautifully appointed rooms that were homey and comfortable.[15]

Following the publication of his previous books, Carl and Karin collaborated on a new book, *Das haus in der sonne*, which immediately became one of the German publishing industry's best sellers of the year—40,000 copies sold in three months, and more than 50 print runs had been produced by 2006.[16]

While Carl's watercolor paintings of his family and home, inspired by Karin, finally brought him the recognition—and money—he sought, he never took to the art form and disparaged watercolors in his memoir. He told anyone who would listen that his fame was not actually due to his beloved watercolors and portraits but to the majestic murals he loved to do. They graced many public buildings in Sweden, and he considered them his lasting legacy. Unbeknownst to most, his wife Karin, an uncelebrated artist, was the creator of those interior designs, the real source of his fame!

One of the few who did appreciate Karin's artistry was Ellen Key, the respected Swedish philosopher, writer, and social reformer, who exclaimed in a Swedish magazine for women and the home, *Idun*, following the 1897 exhibition that too many homes were made ugly by following the decorating principles espoused by the Victorian standards of the day. Her piece, *Skönhet för alla* (Beauty for all), declared that all should have beauty, and she made known her personal social commitment to encouraging lifestyle changes in Sweden.[17]

Key became an advocate of sorts for the unknown textile artist, whom she believed was being overshadowed by her husband. She wrote in her seminal article that Karin was not only the driving force of Carl's creativity but also an impressive "lifestyle" artist in her own right. Key was impressed with the fact that the Larsson children ran throughout the cottage and had dinner with famous guests—something that was unheard of in Sweden and Europe. She admired and advocated for the beautiful and unconstrained clothing worn by Karin and her children, clothing designed by Karin, constructed with fabric that she had woven herself. Key respected and wrote about the informality and brightness of Karin's country home, and more or less announced a brand new trend of freedom in the home to individualize, and create, beauty without artificial stuffiness.[18]

Other influential writers would follow suit, including Gregor Paulsson (1890–1977), author of *Vackrare vardagsvara* (More beautiful things for everyday use), which was published after Carl's death in 1919. These social reformers believed that design was important for everyone, not just the wealthy or influential. Although Paulsson did not single Karin out, he did espouse the design ethos that she was in the process of creating and implementing.[19]

With Karin's designs and Carl's watercolors, the couple had changed the model of family living, and in the process the Larssons changed how the world, particularly the Europeans, viewed domesticity. Karin's home became not simply the ideal for home décor but for lifestyle as well, which we will see was taken up later by IKEA.

In the 1890s Karin had refused to accept the conventions of her day, creating a uniquely individualized environment. Karin's home in Sundborn was her personalized vision of interior design, suited to her own particular family (and not some general norm), that was also revolutionary. But her designs at Lilla Hyttnäs are no longer considered unconventional and eccentric. They are viewed as the epitome of Swedish modern design.

Carl and Karin had looked to the new century not necessarily as the beginning of Carl's fame—which was indeed emerging—but as the start of a simplified, comfortable, country lifestyle for themselves and their children that afforded them much solace, peace, and joy. It was as if after the sadness of losing little Mats everything now would be all right.

Unfortunately, this was not to be the case.

13

The Tragedies, 1905–1916

On New Year's Eve, the church bells of the little Sundborn country chapel rang out across the woods and fields announcing the new year. This turn of the calendar for the new century five years earlier had heralded many changes for Karin, her husband, and her little brood.

First, the new decade produced changes in the small village of Sundborn. A power plant was built between 1900 and 1903 and was situated right next to the Larsson home, so that by 1905 they had electrical power. (Today it still stands next to the current Carl Larsson-Gården.) Carl contributed to the hydroelectric power plant's design, and, in spite of it being a power plant, the building was (and still is) quite beautiful, with industrial architecture not seen other places. There are cornices on the outside edges of the building and decorative windows. It sits on a pond in a beautiful forest setting with tall pine trees and wildflowers growing in abundance.

With the new power plant and electricity coming to the town and to Lilla Hyttnäs, Karin could now use a sewing machine instead of doing her stitch work by hand. Lamps could be electrified, like the one in the formal dining room—a chandelier shaped like a red cactus flower with the wires craftily hidden. But electricity did not seem to change life drastically for the Larssons as renovations continued "on the manse."

Carl's new studio was finally finished—and was it not a kind of church? It was the largest studio in Sweden and, as a monumental muralist, Carl could work on pieces that required a great deal of space. Carl thought of his studio in an ecclesiastical sense, and in celebration he created a few verses of poetry in it:

> Nu ateliern ar fardig, ha hi, ha ha.
> Luftig och! jus och vardig, just sa, just sa.
> Nar hit den lades, pa plan, pa plan.
> Alhnant i socknen sades, fy fan, fy fan.
> Den skimmer hela garden, men dock, men dock,
> lik' fullt har star den, med stock vid stock.[1]

130

This image is of the little country church in Sundborn that the Larsson family attended. Both Karin and Carl are buried there. Nationalmuseum (Stockholm)/ Wikimedia Sverige.

As Carl loved working on large-scale murals, the spaciousness of his home studio allowed for him to work there rather than somewhere outside the home. In the old studio, Karin and Carl had worked side by side, with Carl at his easels and Karin at her loom. It had also functioned as a general "family room" where everyone congregated. And so with the addition of Carl's new studio, Karin now had the old studio to herself. Carl wrote of it, "my wife's handicraft room, where she weaves and spins and stitches."[2]

May was an auspicious month, as Karin had delivered her eighth and last child, son Esbjörn, on May 5, five years earlier. So now with a young child to care for, in addition to the continuous renovations on their home, the upkeep of the garden, the sewing of children's clothes, and the regular interactions with the villagers, Karin's work had to be done around this young child. It was increasingly difficult for her to get any of her own work done. Carl continued to experience moments of despair over professional failures and days of deep depression where blackness emanated from him— sometimes without reprieve. Then, miraculously, he would clear up and be his jovial, entertaining, dynamic self.

Carl painted this image of his youngest son, Esbjörn, in what is called the study corner. Nationalmuseum (Stockholm)/Wikimedia Sverige.

This happy version of Carl had shone on the day of the christening of his children.

Carl, who for years refused to have his children baptized, had a change of heart after the birth of his eighth child. His long-held feelings that religion was unnecessary began to shift: while still hating religion, Carl wanted to be religious. His letters and writings are filled with references to God. Karin by contrast, was balanced in her spirituality. It seems she had a more internal rudder, not necessarily needing a God or a church. She managed to take life in stride, dealing with its vicissitudes without outward expressions of religious faith. Whether that means she was or was not religious is unclear. As to her children's religious life, she apparently went along with this plan of raising unbaptized children. But Carl was feeling more gracious, more generous, and decided a few years after his last son's birth that all the children should be baptized, and he wanted this accomplished in the new studio. Another reason perhaps is that his teen-aged daughter, Suzanne, asked "politely to be baptized."[3]

The children were now growing up and coming into their own. Suzanne, as the eldest, often took care of the other children, and had a personality somewhat like Karin's. She was determined and direct. She apparently had been upset by the household's serving girls who told her that since she was not baptized she could not go to heaven—in fact, saying that she would burn in hell. So she put the request to Carl, that she wanted to be baptized, and he relented.

The dean of the little church in Sundborn, along with many friends and relatives, came to the children's baptism. Karin had decorated the studio with flowers, garlands, and evergreen branches. An altar was set up and each child took their rightful position for the ceremony.

Carl wrote about that day, six months after the birth of his seventh surviving child: "First Suzanne came up to him, her head bent, her eyes cast down, happy and emotional, and she piously received the sacrament. Then the boys, who were at the most awkward age, one of them dour, the other one angry…. Lisbeth, always nice and obedient, reestablished a good impression with her sententious expression and her funny little nose turned downward following the example of her big sister…. Even smaller Kersti— she was only five years old at the time—apparently thought it was some kind of a game, and when she was butted in the back she came bouncing, hop, hop, hop, so cheerful that everybody had to laugh."[4]

Karin was apparently delighted by the proceedings—she and Carl kissed clandestinely behind a closed door. The grandmothers were pleased, and the dean was thrilled to finally have bested Carl. He had complained for years to Carl about his heathen ways.

So with the new studio and the new start for the children, all was going particularly well for the family. Ulf, the eldest son, now 15, was the man of the house when Carl was away. When Carl was home, they worked the land together, chopping trees down and digging in the garden. The other children loved being in Sundborn and in Dalarna where they finally felt as if they had a permanent home.

By 1903 most of Sweden knew of the Larssons through Carl's watercolors, and tourists were descending on their now not-so-little house. The cottage, once a small abode, was finally, after years of Carl and Karin's hard work, a country estate. Over the years there were many renovations, and four extensions had been built on the house.[5]

The large studio, of course, was one extension on the ground floor, which also included additional sleeping rooms at the back of the studio. Over the studio on the first floor, rooms were added for the children and for Karin and Carl's bedrooms.

The home, both inside and out, was used to create a certain lifestyle.

Bouquets of blooms from the outside flowerbeds graced the living spaces inside. The vegetable garden provided ingredients for Karin's sumptuous feasts, frequently assembled for visitors, mostly Carl's friends. No longer was she the timid bride so decried by Eva Bonnier. Nor was she the dreadful cook of her early married years when she couldn't even make porridge. Now she made fabulous meals, with continental flair, using recipes learned from her years in France. She had become a hostess on a grand scale. Karin had designed the rooms in the house that the world now clamored to see because of Carl's watercolors; her creative endeavors continued. She was at her most productive.

This beautiful tapestry, called *Four Elements*, was created in 1903 and was made to fit over a sofa in the new dining room. Courtesy Municipality of Hallsberg.

In January 1904, Karin was immersed in the creation of her first large tapestry which she would name *Four Elements*. She made it to be hung over a sofa in the dining room. The tapestry depicted earth, water, air, and fire in abstract patterns. Karin's textiles were absolutely original. She introduced a new abstract style into her tapestries using vibrant colors and experimenting with Japanese motifs. Technically adventurous, she explored folk techniques and other tapestry techniques as well, such as circular and contour styles, and using colored threads in unique ways.[6] She made the wall hanging in celebration of Carl's 50th birthday and wove it on a Gobelin loom, which was a simple vertical loom she obtained from the Handarbetets Vänner (Friends of Handicraft), which is one of the oldest handicraft and textile institutions in Sweden. It was founded in 1874 at the initiative of Sophie Adlersparre, who was a pioneer of the nineteenth-century women's rights movement in Sweden.[7]

Karin's introduction to textiles, sewing, and domestic arts had come to her via her Aunt Elsie, who had died in 1901, much to the great sadness of Karin, taken by the same condition as her grandfather, Lars—stomach cancer. Aunt Elsie had been devoted to Karin; she had taught her sewing and braiding yarn. This perhaps had been the beginning of several shocking events to come for Karin. (Her aunt had been remembered in an issue of *Idun*, the critical magazine, as an innovative, daring businesswoman, entrepreneur, and supporter of women.)[8]

As Karin was reinventing herself as a textile artist and designer, the commissions, honors, and awards kept coming in for Carl, including the prestigious Egron Lundgren Medal of Honor from the Royal Swedish Academy of Fine Arts. This prize, given annually, was in honor of Lundgren (1815–1875), a Swedish watercolor painter. Carl continued traveling for his various projects and Karin kept weaving and creating tapestries.

Their affectionate relationship continued unabated through letters. At one point Carl asked her to come to him from Sundborn to Stockholm. She replied, "Dearest, sure, I will just do with a little finger wave…. It would be immoral to journey from the maids and seven minor children in order to scare up the money for hotel and restaurants instead of being at home and doing some good."[9]

Work continued on their Sundborn home, both inside and out. A new bridge over the Sundborn creek was built, along with a boat dock. The roof was raised on the second floor, allowing for sleeping quarters under it. The children were growing, and even little Esbjörn was walking. Karin was fully engrossed in the weaving lessons she was taking from the village women. She taught Suzanne to weave as well so that mother and daughter could sit at the loom together and work.[10] Everything seemed very promising. With their publishing enterprises flourishing, and their book, *The Larssons*, being well-received in Germany and other places, both Karin and Carl were happy.[11]

With all this going on—the house renovation, the traveling, the portrait commissions (Carl had just finished a portrait of author Selma Lagerlöf, their friend)—Carl felt the need to retreat somewhere quiet so he could rest as he continued to suffer from debilitating headaches that "gave him bad nights."[12]

But first, there was Christmas to celebrate. Carl and Ulf worked on carpentry jobs outside, where it was cold but bracing for the two outdoorsmen. Suzanne baked bread and on Boxing Day, the day after Christmas, all seven children were at home. The grandmothers visited and there was a feast in the large dining room, cooked by Karin and Suzanne. After dinner there was dancing and music, and the children recited verses and poems.

On Boxing Day, the Swedish upper class would give gifts to the lower classes. The Larssons did this for the many people who worked tirelessly for them: the villagers who became friends; the craftspeople who did carpentry work, painting, and gardening for them; and the young women in the neighborhood who came into the home to take care of the children and who cleaned and cooked. Karin said that she was "proud to see all seven children gathered around the table. I am the happiest woman in the world."[13]

In February of 1905, Carl's mother, Johanna Carolina Erika Ståhlberg, tireless wife of reformed alcoholic Olof Larsson, died at the "ripe old age" of 83. She had been happy in her final years due to Carl's provisions for her and his father. Carl wrote that she did not want to leave this earth, but she did.[14]

And soon it became April, springtime in Sweden—a beautiful time of the year, especially in Sundborn, with the days getting a little longer and the chill in the air disappearing by noon. But the gracious, informal lifestyle of the Larsson family hid the tensions and agonies of its paterfamilias. Carl, always unstable and emotional, was catapulted into a major funk from which he was unable to extricate himself. His work was not going well and he was upset about the loss of his mother.

Then a devastating event occurred.

Ulf, their first-born son and second child, 17 years old, was a happy boy and much admired by his teachers and classmates. It was said of Ulf that when he entered the classroom there was light around him and that he shared this light with others. One day in the beginning of April, his sister, Suzanne, upon returning to Falun from Stockholm, wrote her mother that she was surprised to see that Ulf did not look well. Indeed he had said himself that he was feeling poorly. However, she continued, it did not seem

to be anything seri-
ous—just diarrhea. At
this point there did not
appear to be any reason
for alarm. Carl, how-
ever, was apparently
more worried than
Karin and in a phone
call asked her to go see
Ulf for herself.

While Carl and
Karin lived in Sund-
born, the children lived
near their school in
Falun, first in a rented
apartment, then later in
a house where Carl and
Karin would also live
on occasion. The chil-
dren were taken care of
by Anna Arnbom, one
of the village ladies.
When Karin arrived in
Falun, she took Ulf to
the physician's surgery
for what she thought
was a simple condition,
nothing out of the ordi-
nary. She asked the
doctor how things were
and what needed to be
done for Ulf, who had
told her that he felt
dizzy, but otherwise
seemed healthy and not
weak in any way.

Karin brought Ulf
back to Sundborn to

Ulf and his brother Pontus, painted in watercolor by their father. Nationalmuseum (Stockholm)/Wikimedia Sverige.

recuperate; the family believed that he would be fine. Unfortunately, however, he was quite ill. While recuperating at home, the doctor came to the house and saw that Ulf was not doing well. It was agreed that he should immediately be brought to the hospital in order to have surgery the following day. Carl and Karin were with him until 10 o'clock that first evening Ulf was in the hospital. The doctor thought it would be fine for them to go out and get some air. He told them to enjoy a warm bath and not to be worried.

The first thing in the morning, Karin received a phone call from the hospital saying that Ulf was doing better. But then on the next day, the doctor told her that he was concerned. The day after that, Ulf's condition seemed to get worse, and by the afternoon his health had deteriorated. Karin wrote to her mother, "We thought in the beginning that it was a lovely day." That evening, April 14, 1905, Ulf died of undiagnosed appendicitis.[15]

Carl wrote, "My boy Ulf, my strong and solid oldest son, died as a hero on the operation table, coming there too late due to a mistake by the poor physician. But however limitless the grief seemed, Karin and I grasped hands across the pale body of our eldest son and I said, 'He was ready. There was nothing more for him to do here!' And it was truly a noble heart that had ceased beating."[16]

The funeral of this remarkable young man must have been dreadful. Carl wrote that Ulf's principal attended, together with all his son's classmates and friends, who made a steady procession to the gravesite. Ulf was buried in the Sundborn churchyard.[17]

Karin stayed in Sundborn but was concerned about Carl and advised him to continue with his plans to take a trip through Europe with Anders Zorn and Bruno Liljefors. It was her hope that this trip would help Carl with his profound sorrow.

It did not. He wrote to her from a hotel in Berlin on April 30 that, although he visited the National Gallery and it was impressive, he wanted to come home.

The death of his eldest son was in some ways the beginning of the end for Carl. He seemed unable to go on with life; his melancholy was deep. Karin, as usual, tried to keep Carl's spirits up as well as the spirits of the other children, of her mother and sister Stina in England, and brother Per in Hallsberg—all were grief-stricken by the loss of this young man.

Yet her own grief must have been unimaginable—a mother overcoming the death of a child—still, she carried on. Her letters indicate that she was looking for the goodness in life as she tried to transcend this tragedy. As Lena Rydin wrote, "The death of Ulf in 1905 brought great grief to the home. Nonetheless, Karin was soon back in full swing at her loom. This time she made a cloth to brighten the library, a dark room in which the family often gathered for reading aloud in the evenings. She wove a piece of tapestry and sewed it onto a coarse white cloth. The decorative motif of a stylized insect grasping the black-and-white chequered border was complicated, and Karin was content with only putting it on the visible, short side of the cloth. While Karin was at work on the tapestry one day, her daughter Brita came in eating some fruit. 'Mummy, weave in my pear,' she begged. Karin had a sense of humour and was open to unexpected ideas. The pear was duly incorporated."[18]

Karin wrote to Carl, who was still on his trip, about the children. She told him that Suzanne was at work and that the sun was shining and there was no longer any frost. She told him that they all went to church and then they went out and picked bluebells and in the evening there was dancing. She went on to explain that Pontus was living in "your room, and it is so sweet to have him. Yesterday he was out riding and heard the thrushes play."[19]

This picture of Karin, one of joyful serenity and acceptance following the death of her son, illustrates well the kind of woman she was—a woman who loses a son yet can still revel in the joys of her other children and of nature.

But could it be that in being so caring and protective of Carl that she smothered her own grief?

Carl continued to be overcome with sadness. From Paris he wrote to Karin on May 8, 1905, telling her that he was trying to escape his grief, but that if he did so he would become insane. He assured her that his nature is not to escape things that are sent to him. That he "has never been afraid to be brave."[20]

Carl wrote a poignant passage in *Åt solsidan* (On the sunny side), which one can only assume is about Ulf. "There sits a youth on the seashore and rejoices in the breakers. Then comes a great wave that washes him away and draws him into the depths, and father and mother wring their hands and are never really happy again."[21]

Carl was to struggle with his grief—the two years after Ulf's death were two years of depression, and then there was another blow to endure. During this time, Carl was attacked in public by one of his best friends, August Strindberg. In *En ny blå bok* (A new blue book), published in 1908, Strindberg described Larsson as a man who built his image on a house of cards. He claimed that behind the happy-go-lucky family man was an insecure and mean-spirited artist.

Worst of all, Strindberg also took aim at Larsson's wife, calling her a frustrated painter and a nasty devil. He wrote that while she was always depicted as sober and compliant, in reality she was actually controlling and furious that Carl had made her give up her own career as an artist. Strindberg declared that Karin drove Carl to illustrate their family life in Sundborn, with Karin and the lovely cottage as the centerpiece. He said that because she had been forced to give up her own career by her husband, she controlled and manipulated him into painting pictures of her and their family domain.

Carl reacted to this as a devastating betrayal. What was most upsetting to him was that he thought he and Strindberg were best friends, even though Carl knew that August had faults—that he could be a dangerous person. After the publication of Strindberg's vicious attack, Carl wanted to kill him. He actually walked around Stockholm carrying an expensive knife given to him by Anders Zorn, stalking Strindberg, who he was prepared to stab with that knife.

Carl did not act on his plan to murder Strindberg, but the situation between them made Carl "sick for a couple of years." He wrote that his entire nervous system was shattered.[22]

Perhaps it was professional jealousy on Strindberg's part, but it could also have been that there were years of tension between the two. It is also clear that Strindberg, somewhat like Carl himself, held grudges, wrote awful things about friends and foes alike, and seemed to have a personality that was not practically joyful or happy. Perhaps there was an element of personal jealousy to his diatribe as well. He did not have a happy married life, which, for all their issues and problems, Karin and Carl did.

Carl continued to be furious with Strindberg, "that terrible man" who wrote those awful things about the Larsson family. Strindberg's book would continue to anger Carl for many years after its publication. It angered and hurt Karin as well.

Soon after the Strindberg fiasco, Carl was hit with another blow. In 1911 his father, whom he had hated growing up, died. This was the third recent family burial Carl witnessed, after his mother and his son. His father was 87 years old and had felt at home in the house that Carl bought for him—Kartbacken.

Carl did his best with his family. He fulfilled his duties to his parents, even though he still had issues with his father. He wrote, "God be praised that I could bring some joy into the lives of these people who had seen so much suffering!"[23]

But then another blow:

In her declining years, Hilda had returned to Hallsberg and lived with her friend, Anna Wilhelmson, the sister of the painter Carl Wilhelmson. She was close to Per and Anna, who lived in the house that Adolf built (which Hilda and Adolf had never lived in), and Per had continued to run Adolf's business. Hilda never seemed ill and, according to Carl, "spent her time with extensive studies of geography, acquired stereoscope photographs from all over the world, studied them in conjunction with all the travel books of the world." She thus became the most traveled woman in the world. But then one evening after a large dinner of lobster and other foods that were hard to digest, she fell ill.[24]

Karin spent time with her mother at the end of her life not believing that she would die, only that she was ill; nonetheless, Hilda died on April 7, 1913. Carl was traveling at the time in Germany and France and so, once again left alone to handle difficulties, Karin had to deal with the death of her beloved mother on her own.[25] Now Karin was the old guard and she was waiting for the next death—perhaps Carl's.

But then things turned around for the Larssons momentarily on May 25, 1913—Carl's 60th birthday. *Idun*, a magazine published in Sweden from 1887 until 1963, published an entire issue devoted to Carl, *Faluns Carl Larsson nummer*. The magazine, subtitled *A Practical Weekly Magazine for Women and the Home*, focused on literature and gender equality. You might say that it was the pinnacle of Carl's career to have a full edition of *Idun* devoted to him. Many wrote articles for the edition praising Carl, but the highlight was an article titled "A Letter from Wife Karin Larsson."[26]

Karin begins her tribute to Carl by acknowledging that she had had a minimal concept of home and hearth when they were first married and praises her husband for his patience in accepting these domestic limitations.

She tells of a time early in their marriage when Carl and a friend invited people to their cottage in Grez for a Christmas party, and Karin hardly knew how to boil water. She ends by thanking Carl for all he has done for her.

As Carl celebrated his 60th birthday—Karin was only 54—she recognized that she had come a long way in the years that they had been married. She was no longer a frustrated artist, nor a neophyte homemaker. She was a woman of the world, a mother, and the wife of a famous artist—a woman who, one could say, was responsible for the happiness and professional accomplishments of her husband.

Perhaps she wondered what the years ahead would have in store for him—and for her.

14

From Muse to Mother,
1917–1918

It feels good to sit here in our little cabin ... my memories are my greatest treasures, also the most painful.—Karin Larsson's journal

During World War I, Sweden held onto its long-standing policy of neutrality, but this did not dispel Sweden's anxiety—nor Karin's. Sweden, at that time and during World War II, had a strong affinity and shared cultural links with Germany. King Gustaf V had married the granddaughter of Kaiser Wilhelm I. So while Sweden was ostensibly neutral, it had allegiance to Germany. The Larssons did as well, since one of Karin and Carl's daughters was engaged to a German, and any grandchildren from that union would be Germans.[1]

The entry of the United States into the war on the side of the Allies in early 1917 greatly increased the pressure on Sweden to conclude an agreement on trade and shipping favorable to the Allied powers. One specific request was that the Swedish reduce their iron-ore exports to Germany in return for increased supplies of food from the Allies—Sweden's food supply had become increasingly low due to the Allied blockade.[2]

The international agitation contributed to Karin's generalized fear about the war, which she expressed outwardly within the family. This was unusual for her. She had always been a woman who contained negative emotions within herself—unlike her husband who was never able to contain anything, let alone his fears and anxieties. Although at times the war seemed far away, it was recounted in the daily papers, so in Sundborn there was a sense of war somewhere out there. This war was unsettling to Karin as she and Carl had a son-in-law who had just returned from the German front lines.

Perhaps it was because Karin followed world history carefully that she was more susceptible to worry about the world beyond her little village.

She had lived all over Europe and traveled regularly to Great Britain to see her sister. She had read about the Boer's brave battle in South Africa and the rise of Japan, which had fomented tensions in Russia. This was all before the start of the war. Now that the war was raging, the conflagration was raging inside Karin, too; her anxiety was almost overwhelming her.

Throughout the war, however, Karin continued to be proactive, refusing to give in to her fears. She and other women in the village knitted warm clothes for the soldiers for the Swedish Red Cross, but while Karin knitted "she pondered," her mind as active as her moving fingers. She was especially happy to knit a cape, which could be used as both coat and blanket for those poor boys at the front. Karin frequently talked about her admiration for Elsa Brändström (1888–1948), known both as the "Angel of Siberia" and the Florence Nightingale of Sweden, who went to Siberia as part of her work for the Swedish Red Cross.[3,4]

By this time, Karin had been married to Carl for 35 years and her family was famous across Europe. After years of expansion, their once-small cottage, Lilla Hyttnäs, had become a country estate and was perhaps the most well-known home in Europe, especially in Germany (and of course in Sweden). But this fame was not good enough for Carl. Some of Carl's tensions had to do with the war, of course; unlike Karin, however, who was worried for the world, for Sweden, and for her family, Carl seemed to be concerned mostly with his reputation and his finances, which had never been better. He was fearful that this war might diminish his bank account, which he was counting on to provide for him and Karin in their old age.

Carl was still working as a painter, but Karin's work as a designer and textile artist was somewhat over now that the cottage in Lilla Hyttnäs was completely renovated. And so her artistic life, which began when she was eight or nine, was now in many ways secondary to her worthy and significant role as mother and housekeeper to so many children—and to her husband. In her late 40s, Karin found that it was the lives of her children that were of greatest interest to her—even though for Carl, it seemed as if his work was of greatest interest to him. For her part, Karin saw herself in these years as the devoted mother and grandmother. Her children were mostly grown up now and doing well, and she was always happiest when they came to visit.

In these later years of her life, Karin would reflect on the life she had had with her children: how stumbling and ineffective she had been as both mother and housekeeper in those early days of her marriage in Grez. Poor Suzanne! She had the misfortune of being born first and was the recipient of Karin's unsure first maternal steps. But by all accounts, Suzanne and

Karin had a strong relationship, and Karin's lack of experience with her did not do any lasting harm.

She frequently thought about the children she had lost: her beloved Ulf and the baby Mats, who had died a few months after his birth in 1885. Karin always felt a sense that she had not done enough, known enough, to keep him alive. Even as she thought this, she also knew that there was nothing she could have done to prevent this loss, as his death had no discernable cause.

But Ulf, dear Ulf, to have had him for 18 years and then to have lost him because of that foolish medical error. After all this time, it was still hard to believe. Ulf, their second born, would have been in his late 20s by then and perhaps embroiled in this dreadful war had he lived. He would have been a great man, Karin knew, and she had moments of sadness when she thought of him. But then, ever the optimist, she would remind herself of the rich 18 years they spent together.

And what of the other children? How many of them became artists like their mother and father? The answer is none of them! By 1917 the children were leaving home and experimenting with life. Suzanne had married a physician, and she and her husband came back to Sundborn frequently. Pontus, the third-born and second son, was also married and became an engineer at a separator plant. Karin and Carl understood that he was very well liked and highly valued.[5]

Lisbeth was living in Ramlösa, Sweden, and worked as a physical therapist, while her sister, Brita, lived in Bremen, Germany, adding another layer of fear to Karin's worries. Brita was also a therapist—and a volunteer for the German Red Cross. She corresponded frequently with her parents, telling them of all the good food that the nice patients offered her. On her days off, she was happy, she told them, to take little trips to see her fiancé, Gustav Friederich, in Stralsund, Germany, where he was doing his *Kriegsdienst* (military service). Gustav had been ill since returning from the eastern front in Russia. At the moment, he was training recruits as he recovered, but Karin feared that he soon would be sent back to the front.[6]

Then there was Kersti, next in line, who had brightened their lives after the loss of Mats. She was now a bit of a worry to Karin, however, as she had bouts of ill health. Recovering in Sundborn with her parents, she was responsible for taking care of the garden, and she loved playing the piano in the evening to the delight of both her parents.[7]

Esbjörn, their youngest, a farmhand, still loved being in Sundborn pulling up crayfish from the swiftly flowing creek behind their house. He was 17 and would soon graduate from secondary school. He would then continue with his career as a farmer like his ancestors before him—or, as

Carl told Karin, perhaps he would train himself to be a colonizer in Africa or the Orient.[8]

Karin's relationship with the children was maintained through letters—she wrote to all of them constantly, it seemed. She could kid them, challenge them, and chastise them all in the same missive. In one letter to Brita dated May 10, 1917, for her birthday, Karin wrote from Falun, "Dear little child, you made me sad, angry, furious. But above all worried, worried!!"[9]

If she did not hear from her children, she was doubly upset—uncharacteristically so. In one letter to Kersti, Karin wrote asking why she had not written to her, "You must believe I was sad and ashamed when Emma [Zorn] on the phone said yes that she had letters from Signe." How disconcerting it was for Karin that her friend clearly had a daughter who was more dutiful than her own with regards to correspondence.

In a more even letter to Brita from Falun on May 28, 1917, she wrote, "Dear little girl, now I sit here in your little room, which is broiling hot. I am escaping from Sundborn.... I need to spray fruit trees.... I consider it my civic duty this summer to attempt to engage myself seriously in the garden. Yours, for all the good advice. Thankfully, Mother."[10]

Now that all of the children, except for their youngest, were gone, Karin and Carl liked to spend time alone, which they did at their farm in Falun, the farm they had purchased in 1907 to live in during the academic year when their children attended school in the city. The following year they acquired a neighboring farm and used the little cottage there as a graphic workshop and guest cottage. They would travel from the little Falun cottage to the home in Sundborn, primarily when the older children were home or when they received visiting relatives and friends. Their large country estate in Sundborn was different from their small house on the outskirts of Falun. The home in Sundborn was more for the family; this little cottage in the city was just for them. It was not pictured throughout Europe, but was a private haven. And Karin, being a very private person, needed this haven.

Carl and Karin often walked the centuries-old trail through the woods from the Falun cottage to Sundborn. It cut through the forest and over hills. For years Karin and the children had taken this way into the city rather than use a horse and carriage on the highway. These walks from city to village and back again gave Karin some escape from her fears.[11]

At this point, Karin was not taking her young children to pick flowers and fruit in the forest, but her grandchildren. She loved being at Sundborn with them. And she would travel to pick them up and bring them back to the country estate, often by train. Karin liked walking about Sundborn with

Carl, too, who, now that he was older and famous, would finally give Karin a bit of the respect that she deserved. He would point to her when they were out walking passing neighbors as if to say, "she did it; it was her." And indeed, there were times when he publicly gave her recognition for all that she had done for him as muse and model, such as in his memoirs where he said that his wife and children were his preferred models. But more than that, theirs was a love affair. Carl wrote, "God in His Goodness has blessed me to the fullest with the treasures of earthly goods. My wife is certainly one of His angels, and to me she's as earthly as she is indispensable in running a simple household and seeing to it that the children are clean and kept in line. But when Karin cowers in a corner as the shades of night are falling and all I can see of her is her round, dreamy eyes peering out at me from the deep shadows, so full of unswerving affection and abiding love, that's when I fall at her feet, bury my ugly bald head in her lap and feel myself drift away with her."[12]

And what of Carl during these declining years?

Reflecting on his past, Carl was sometimes able to believe what he wrote, that he had a good life! But his lifelong depression was now producing physical symptoms such as migraines, which affected his eyes. This affliction was bothering him more and more.[13]

Karin was *mor* (mother) to her children and *mormor* (grandmother) to her grandchildren, but what to Carl now that her days as muse and model were mostly over? Sometimes she was a mother to him also, but if not that, certainly a caretaker. He had been unwell for some time but tried not to let anyone know. He continued to paint when he could, but he often let the paintbrush fall to the floor.

In those final months of 1918, Karin worked on one final sewing project, which she planned to give to Carl. From the beginning she called it the "World War I Pillow." And as the waning months of 1918 came to an end, Karin and Carl moved into a different space in their life and marriage. Karin thought that Carl would settle down. Perhaps, he told Karin, he would write his memoirs. They would finally lead the peaceful life in the country he promised. Now there would be no need to travel all over Europe. They could simply enjoy each other and grow old together, gracefully and quietly in Sundborn and in Falun.

But that was not to be.

15

Widowhood, 1919–1928

The previous few years had been perhaps the most difficult of Karin's many years of marriage—and of life. Of course there was Ulf's death and the war, and Aunt Lisen's death, but also the loss of Karin's mother in 1913, from which Karin was still bereaved and grieving. Hilda had always been there for her daughter, through all her years and transitions—at the French School, during her stay in Paris, and then in her marriage to Carl. It was always to Hilda that Karin turned, for her mother mirrored Karin's own resolute determination.[1,2]

For these years had also seen the acceleration of Carl's ill health, his professional humiliation, and his unremitting sorrow at his son's death—which Karin felt, too, but processed differently. Never without ailments throughout their marriage, now at age 65, Carl appeared to be at his worst, with incapacitating headaches, eye problems, depression, inexplicable rashes, and exhaustion. As Carl wrote following the Strindberg episode, "My entire nervous system was shattered."[3]

Through it all Karin had, as was customary for wives of that time and place, stood stalwart and courageous within the confines of her marriage to Sweden's famous and beloved artist.

Somehow Karin feared that perhaps her husband didn't even want to live. He was refusing to paint portraits of the famous people who clamored after him—even portraits like the one commissioned by his good friend, novelist Selma Lagerlöf. But he felt that he just could not paint, regardless of the potential commissions.

Perhaps the proverbial straw that broke the strong camel's back became one travail that was Carl's alone to endure. There was nothing Karin could do to alleviate his distress or fix this problem. He had been granted, finally after years of proposals to the Swedish government, a commission on his final huge mural, *Midvinterblot* (Midwinter Sacrifice). The mural was to grace the walls above the grand staircase of Stockholm's famous and well-regarded Nationalmuseum. The work took many years to complete, with

Midvinterblot (Midwinter Sacrifice). **Nationalmuseum (Stockholm)/Wikimedia Sverige.**

excruciating revisions executed by the frustrated artist amidst much deliberation by the museum's artistic committee. The mural was ultimately rejected.

Carl told anyone who would listen that his prestige and fame was not due to the beloved watercolors and portraits of his family and his home, but to the majestic murals he loved to create. Indeed, his murals did grace many public buildings throughout Sweden, and he considered them his legacy. However, it was *Midvinterblot* that was his crowning glory, the final pearl of his artistic necklace. Its rejection devastated him.[4]

He wrote with his usual bravado nonetheless: "The fate of the *Midwinter Sacrifice* broke me! This I admit with a dark anger. And still, it was probably the best thing that could have happened, for now my intuition tells me—again—that with all its weakness, this painting will one day be honoured with far better placement after my death."[5]

It was eventually sold to a Japanese collector, but today it is in its rightful place in the grand stairway of the Nationalmuseum. And it would be Karin who made that happen. This shy grandmother, a few years before she died, went before the so-called museum lords—she had to take bromine tablets beforehand to calm herself—and saw to it that the painting came back to the Nationalmuseum in Stockholm in 1926, after Carl's death.[6]

Frieberg wrote that for Carl to have his final and (to Carl's mind) greatest work rejected, seized him with a fatigue whose nature he had never known before.[7] And would not know again.

The debilitating events of the previous years completely overshadowed Carl's many years of success and called upon Karin's greatest tact and diplomacy as she attempted to pull him out of his funk. Although during this time he received gifts, money, awards, and prizes (shortly after the *Midvinterblot* fiasco he received the prestigious Berlin Prize), he could not be calmed. He retired to Lilla Hyttnäs, although he was only happy there when the children were visiting, taking breaks from their various personal and professional responsibilities.

As his melancholy deepened, and because he could no longer paint, in the spring of 1918, Carl decided to turn to those memoirs that he had told Karin he felt a need to write. Although such efforts would surely be cathartic to Carl, the results would be hurtful to Karin; nevertheless, she said nothing to stop him.

In his memoir called *Jag* (Myself), Carl revealed the details of his early life for the first time. He described his upbringing in the Stockholm ghetto with an alcoholic father who abandoned the family and a tireless mother, the loss of his brother at a young age, and his role, beginning at age 13, as family breadwinner.

He also described his depressive, neurotic nature, which to the casual viewer would have seemed at odds with the bucolic, happy watercolors he created of his home life. Through these descriptions of his mental agonies, people would realize for the first time what Karin must have put up with all those years.

Surely most devastating for Karin, however, were his revelations of his repugnance for the famous paintings of Lilla Hyttnäs for which he had become justly famous—and wealthy. Those magnificent, bucolic scenes articulating the graceful, informal Larsson way of life that thrilled Europeans disgusted Carl in his final years. At the end of his life, he was thinking of his legacy, and he did not think the watercolors of his family life were a suitable tribute to his artistry—he wanted to be remembered for his epic murals.

Karin merely stood by as Carl bared his soul. Although she had overseen most of his artistic endeavors for many years, she left this one to him. Daughter of a wealthy entrepreneur and a cultured and educated housewife, Karin herself was a shy, private, hardworking, and sober woman who had lived for many years with the eccentricities, celebrity, and grandiosity of her husband—in the shadows where she liked to be.

Because of their marriage, she had given up her own career as a painter in order to provide Carl with the emotional support, financial stability, and artistic guidance that he needed in order to create. Now, in his dark and gloomy final years, he was deteriorating. His energy ebbed, his desire to paint dissipated, and his anger was unbearable and debilitating.

Karin had long provided Carl with an environment that allowed him to do as he pleased, such as taking commissions that removed him from family life and taking Karin away from their children to accompany him all over Europe. She worked so hard to provide joy, humor, and contentment not only to Carl but to their entire family. Now, in this autobiography he was determined to write, Carl was laying bare the real Carl and, by extension, the real Larsson family. She was not happy to have family secrets made public, but as usual Karin acquiesced.

Karin enjoyed writing, even though she still had trouble with word choice and organizing her thoughts. From a very early age, she had been considered by her family to be a gifted writer, despite all of her problems. She eventually became a prolific letter-writer and religiously kept a *dagbok* (journal) in which she wrote about her daily life, copied recipes, and wrote movingly about her joys and her sadnesses. But she never contemplated publishing it; given that she was half of a famous couple, it would not only have been publishable but marketable as well.

Carl had told himself that he was suffering for his sins, bad deeds done, either in this existence or a previous one. If he could only do his penance, then the pains would go away. Indeed, nearing the end of writing his autobiography—his confession, if not his penance—he did feel better. He "woke on the morning he had finished the book, without the headache for the first time in a long time."[8]

Now, Karin thought, with this finished, they would resume walking arm and arm down the dusty paths of Sundborn and through the busy streets of Falun. And indeed for a few days they did. Many said that, for the first time, he openly acknowledged his wife. Even in his memoirs, he acknowledged, seemingly with some regret, that it was her idea for him to paint watercolors of their home. It was difficult for Carl to publicly acknowledge the value his wife created for him professionally. He could certainly wax eloquent on how grand she was and how she had changed his life, but he had always been hesitant to give the credit due to her for decorating their home, creating a lifestyle, and mentoring him as a painter. Lena Rydin claimed "he consistently took a dominant attitude in public. It was his home and his work. In this respect, he was a man of his times."[9]

He also understood that he was a man of substance; he was finally able to acknowledge his economic stability. He had not "felt a knife on [his] throat, an economical knife"[10] for a long time. Much of their wealth had come not from Carl's earnings, though those had increased in the previous 15 years, but from Karin's family, who had supported them in the lean, early years of their marriage. Now, however, in their later years, Carl was self-supporting.

According to Bo Lindell:

> Carl Larsson would never have settled down into middle-class security if he had not found safe anchorage through his marriage. It was his wife who provided him with the social prestige that was needed; it was she who created about him the harmonious environment that he was then to perpetuate in his entire life. What she meant to him when it came to smoothing the way in self-sacrifice and self-effacement, banishing difficulties and inspiring and encouraging, we can only infer. Without her Carl Larsson would hardly have found the peace for working that made it possible for him to create a parade of remarkable works. It was she who enabled Carl Larsson to maintain so long his belief in happiness, the happiness he wanted to share with others when he painted the watercolors for *Ett hem*.[11]

Carl and Karin now lived mostly in their little cottage in Falun, a few miles from their now famous Sundborn home. He called it "our own house, at the very outskirts of the town, among the poor ones, where I feel most at home."[12]

None of this took into account Karin's desires or sensibilities—she was seemingly always at the service of Carl. Yet it was Karin who had designed the house and its furnishings and who had made slipcovers, drapes, bed hangings, furniture, and clothes for herself and the children that were copied all over Europe. "Art historians," wrote Hans-Curt Köster, "are agreed that the creation of their Sundborn home was chiefly if not practically exclusively the work of Karin, though Carl did have a hand in it."[13]

So while Carl articulated his feeling of release from pain and depression upon completion of his book, Karin felt otherwise. She was not happy about his writing for an audience about the inner workings of his mind—and the outer workings of his relationship with her and their children. The children, too, were very unhappy with the thought that their father might publish his memoirs. Still, like the rest of Sweden, they celebrated the New Year and Karin must have hoped it would bring peace and good cheer to her husband. But did it? At the end of his book, he wrote: "My last chapter was listless and shallow. I held back. I closed off the flow of feelings, was not willing to give all of me. I ask myself, why? How should it really have been? Perhaps, after all, just as it was? For, my friend, surely you could guess what was going on in my life when I thought I was writing the last lines of my life's history."[14]

January 22, 1919, was cold and windy; night encroached early. The Swedish sun had set by three o'clock that afternoon. They were gathered in the studio: Karin and Carl were sitting on the sofa reading, while Brita, who was 26 at the time, played the piano. Kersti, preparing for a ball at the Royal Community Parliament Officers Mess, was told by her father how beautiful she looked before she stepped out into the cold night. He compared her to a Christian Eriksson sculpture. Carl and Karin continued to sit quietly in the studio listening to Brita at the piano. Shortly thereafter they went upstairs to their sitting room.[15]

While Karin was seated beside Carl, who was lying on his bed, he abruptly whispered, "Karin! Jag dör!" (Karin, I die!). And with that, Carl passed away from what would today be diagnosed as a massive stroke.[16]

Immediately following Carl's death, Karin sat mute in the pale January dawn. She later told her son-in-law that she heard the church bells from Grez ringing—the French bells that she loved. The bells brought her peace, gratitude, and joy. Karin always saw things in the most positive light, even the death of her beloved spouse. In the morning, she said to her girls that she knew she would see him again, but today and in the foreseeable future she would not see him—only in the afterlife would they be reunited.[17]

By midday the news of the death of Carl Larsson rang out over the country and far beyond its borders. The *Svenska Dagladet*, Stockholm's morning paper, called Larsson's death a national tragedy.[18] The *Göteborgs-Possten* called him "our most beloved artist."[19]

Frieberg related that Karin wore her mourning in a beautiful and distinctive way, but otherwise showed no outward signs of grief. Yet her body seemed more bent, her chest more shrunken. Many of their friends came to Karin or wrote to her. At the funeral service for Carl, held at the Sundborn *kyrka* (church) a few days later, Karin's wise eyes met the eyes of others with calm. No one dared to come up to her with condolences because they did not want to break her serenity. She was able to hold herself together, provided no one came too close to her grief.[20]

Karin's journal reveals some of her thoughts about living without Carl. In the days and months following his death, she never felt that Carl actually left her. She always felt as if he were with her. The love affair was complete until the end, and even after the end.

Later, back in Sundborn on April 13, 1919, she wrote, "Here the sun shines, it dips from the roof; the birds chirp. So strange! I thought that the gray winter day you gave us would never fade."[21]

But there was still the matter of Carl's memoirs that he had been desperate to have published.

When Karin and Karl Otto Bonnier sat down together to read Carl's autobiography, they were shaken and chose to put the lid back on this Pandora's box. The children were also upset when they read it. One of the reasons was certainly his recounting of his premarital love stories—primarily with Wilhelmina Holmgren and the loss of his two children by her—and his relationship with French model Gabrielle. Karin stressed to the family that these experiences had nevertheless made Carl the man he was.

It would be 12 years later—four years after Karin Larsson's death—when Bonnier would publish the autobiography. Before she died, Karin wrote a coda to his book saying, "Two days after my beloved husband finished his memoirs [he had completed them in September but put finishing touches to them right before he died], and before he had time to polish them artistically, the saga of his life ended forever. The saga of the great loving heart that never judged or condemned because he had himself experienced all the misery of a life. The saga of the victorious spirit. The saga of a human being."[22]

At some point, someone suggested that she work with a medium to contact Carl. She told this friend, "We have never been those who wanted to peep through the veil to see what's on the other side. If Carl had wanted something told me he would come to me directly. We have never had any secrets from each other, not ever. Nor do we need an intermediary."[23]

Karin continued to be busy. She traveled and took care of her beloved grandchildren, and, while she missed her husband, she lived without him as she had lived with him, with optimism and grace of spirit—and humor. She wrote one day in May 1921, "Spring is in its purest budding, rye and wheat color is the greenest green and the water is blue. The sun is as only an Indian painter can paint it. In the air, there is the singing of an invisible lark. I know me to not be older than before, but in the mirror I face a very old and wrinkled face."[24]

One winter's evening in February 1928, when Karin was staying with her son, Esbjörn, at his farm in Södermanland, she telephoned her daughters before going to bed. That night she died peacefully at 68 years old without a lot of fuss, just as she had lived. She is buried beside Carl Larsson in the church graveyard in Sundborn.

When Carl Larsson's memoirs were published, they were coldly received by a public that no longer revered him. Many art critics felt that they had been deluded by Carl's famous home scenes, which show only the happy side of his life. He was accused of "pumping life into a myth."[25]

By this time, not only was Carl's reputation in tatters, but his home was falling apart. The beautiful Sundborn hut-turned-mansion was run-down and shabby. It had almost become a ghost home. But Lilla Hyttnäs would rise from the ashes of Carl's disreputable memoir—and Karin would gain the respect and accolades that she never sought but so richly deserved.

However, it would take until 1997, 69 years after Karin's death, for this reversal of fortune to take place.

16

The Legacy, 1929–Present

Following the death of Karin Larsson in 1928, the Larssons were all but forgotten—and somewhat devalued by the publication of Carl's autobiography, *Jag* (Myself). However, in 1930 the Stockholm Exhibition, organized by the Swedish Society for Industrial Design, mounted a show for international audiences with the goal of displaying the works of Swedish artists in glass, furniture, fabric, and industrial and interior design. While not showcasing the Larssons specifically, the exhibition did create excitement for and interest in Swedish design once again by highlighting the large windows, clean surfaces, fabrics and textiles inspired by folklore, and spartan décor—those design elements utilized by Karin. This was perhaps one of the most influential design exhibitions in Sweden, with more than four million visitors.[1]

Then, two and a half decades later in 1955, the Home Exhibition, or H55 as it was also called, a Bureau of International Expositions (BIE), recognized as a world's fair held in the town of Bie in southern Sweden, cemented the foundations of contemporary Swedish design. One of the highlights of this exhibition was the everyday sitting room for daily socializing, which brought to mind Karin Larsson's drawing room—her Swedish room.[2]

In the meantime, the children of Carl and Karin tried to both revive the memory of their parents as well as restore their homestead. In 1936 they unsuccessfully attempted to convince the Swedish government to purchase Lilla Hyttnäs to use as an historical site, using revenue from the national lottery. When the government refused, the family joined together and used their own funds to open the estate to the public on a regular basis. In 1943 they formed the Carl Larsson Family Association, under whose auspices the family owned and operated Lilla Hyttnäs as a museum.[3]

Today the family continues to use the structure, grounds, and buildings as a home, not just a museum, with the family holding an annual "family

155

only" meeting in August to determine the fate and activities of the home. The Family Association, today with approximately 250 members—all of whom have a kinship with the famous couple—is run now by great grandchildren and great-great grandchildren. The homestead functions as a museum, with some 60,000 people per year from all over the world coming to the tiny village of Sundborn and the grounds of the family estate. This causes some problems because of wear and tear on the magnificent textiles created by Karin, as well as on the furnishings and other aspects of the house. And in fact, the textiles, rugs, wall hangings, and bed coverings have been stored for posterity, with seamstresses creating new versions of Karin's famous designs. The estate is well-kept now, both the grounds and home. There is a gift shop, and tours are provided daily throughout the house.

It wasn't until 1997, however, that the world finally found Karin Larsson.

In the autumn of 1997, 100 years from that rainy summer in Sundborn when the Larsson family embarked on their new life at Lilla Hyttnäs, Karin finally stepped out of the large shadow cast by her neurotic and demanding husband. She became an icon in her own right.

IKEA, the Swedish home furnishing chain, mounted a display at the Victoria and Albert Museum in London that highlighted Karin's work as never before in an exhibition titled "Carl and Karin Larsson: Creators of the Swedish Style." As part of the museum's *Great Designer Series*, the exhibition showcased Karin—not as Carl's wife—but as a Swedish innovator, one whose artistry was based on the native crafts and folklore of Dalarna, the province where she lived and created.[4]

The event, the first ever major exhibition held outside Sweden on the Larssons' work, was widely and favorably reviewed in the British press and on radio and television, and positive reviews also appeared in other European media. Needless to say, the display aroused considerable interest in Sweden as well, since the profiled designers had fallen out of favor after their deaths.[5]

This exhibition gave prominent attention to Lilla Hyttnäs, characterizing Karin as its designer, rather than emphasizing Carl's contributions. For the first time, the show brought international attention to the obscure creator of a style that continues to have an extraordinary impact on interior design. From the *V & A*, the conservatory newsletter of the Victoria and Albert Museum, "When the holiday cottage became the permanent home for their large family, it was enlarged and transformed. In total contrast to the prevailing style of dark heavy furnishings, its bright interiors incorporated an innovative blend of Swedish folk design and fin de siècle influences, including Japonisme and Arts and Crafts ideas from Britain. The Larssons created a style of interior decoration recognized as quintessentially Swedish with colorfully painted furniture and woven textiles. Karin designed and produced the textiles and her loom is one of the objects in the exhibition. Through Carl's watercolors of his house and family, the couple's ideas on interior design reached a large audience."[6]

The show exhibited re-creations of five rooms, including the kitchen, dining room, studio, old room, and miner's cottage, and (to particular effect) that beautiful drawing room that Carl illustrated during that rainy season—his watercolor "breakthrough." The rooms were all created with original furniture and fittings from the famous cottage in Sundborn. Visitors were able to experience life as the inhabitants of Lilla Hyttnäs lived it. Walking through the exhibition and viewing the more than 300 objects—photographs of the children and of Karin and Carl; furniture, such as that famous rocker that Karin designed; textiles she wove into tablecloths and bedclothing; and the books that the family read together—revealed to a wide audience the Larssons' relatively iconic way of life.[7]

Now these informal rooms and their attendant country lifestyle are emulated in antique shops around the world, and, according to an article in *The Economist*, the designs strike a resoundingly contemporary note: this informal country lifestyle resembles the modern country look seen in so many magazines.[8]

The clean and iconic designs of Karin, from the white hardwood construction of Danish modern furniture to the simple furnishings and the woven and embroidered textiles, made their way into homes across the globe. The informal style, replacing the stuffiness of formal dining and living rooms, is now seen in homes around the world. Eleish and Van Breens, authors of design and interior decorators themselves, have said that Karin and Carl's home "was a revolutionary design statement at the time. They furnished the rooms with folk décor deemed unfashionable at the time, that they painted in daring, bold colors. In fact, every surface of the house is brightly painted and the overall effect is sunny and light."[9]

Karin's rooms and designs had a major impact on ordinary homemakers, and ultimately caused the final move toward design theories of Scandinavia in the field of interior design—from a Victorian sensibility to a more modern Swedish ethos. Michael Snodin, one of the editors (along with Elisabet Stavenow-Hidemark) of the design book, *Carl and Karin Larsson: Creators of the Swedish Style*, wrote: "certain artists have the ability to spread gold dust on the wintry path of life. The Larssons were such artists. Their vision of Swedishness is more firmly embedded in the national psyche even than the Swedish sense of community. To have a lilac-embowered cottage in the country in your family's place of origin—that is the Swedish dream. To have it light and white, clean and airy, like a summer meadow sprinkled with ox-eyed daisies, is the very essence of that dream."[10]

Karin's "Swedish dream" and its groundbreaking impact came to light only after a number of decades of shifting artistic sensibilities, and largely due to the efforts of an enterprising young Swede, Ingvar Kamprad.

Born on the outskirts of Älmhult on March 30, 1926, Kamprad began his sales career at age 14, riding his bicycle around the Swedish countryside, selling matches that he bought in bulk from a supplier in Stockholm. Eventually he sold other small goods such as fish, seeds, pens, pencils, holiday cards, and tree ornaments.[11]

It has been said of Kamprad that because he had dyslexia—as Karin was thought to have had—he had to make a special effort to accomplish his goals. Perhaps that is why he went into business for himself. He may have felt it would have been too difficult to work for anyone else. With money given to him by his father, he eventually opened a small store in Älmhult in 1943, which he called IKEA: IK from his name, plus E for Elmtaryd, the farm he grew up on, and A for his small village, Agunnaryd. (Interestingly, the acronym IKEA is similar to the Greek word for home [οικία] and to the Finnish word meaning correct or right [oikea].)[12]

So how did the frugal and innovative retailer, born roughly around the time Karin Larsson died, make the leap to design? And how did IKEA make a connection with consumers worldwide through Karin's design sensibility?

To understand this we have to remember that Karin and Carl's visual imagery, along with Karin's innovative designs, did much to establish the widespread idea of the Larsson family's domestic design and lifestyle throughout Sweden. The yearly IKEA catalogue illustrates middle-class values (almost a religion to Kamprad), but imbedded in this religiosity is an egalitarian sensibility that was consistent with the way the Larssons broke with the Victorian code and led a freer, more family-focused life in the airy, sun-filled rooms of their cottage estate.

IKEA appropriated the Larsson style: the bright, plant-filled rooms with spare furnishings in the style of an elegant farmhouse. These objects and images are seen today not only with the furnishing and design ideals of IKEA, but they also define a lifestyle that the IKEA philosophy encourages: be somewhat casual and ruleless, assemble your own furniture, and pull things together yourself to create informal, simplified, and modest interiors.

Of course the main difference between the Larssons and the modern-day IKEA customer is that the Larssons were not into prepackaged design. Karin, a revolutionary interior designer and furniture maker, established her magical style through her own creativity. She designed her own furniture and painted chairs and tables in colors that she liked. Karin wove fabrics whose designs and ideas came directly from Swedish folklore. She was the inventor. To do this, Karin had to think independently, take risks, and be unconcerned with what the neighbors thought. IKEA took those ideas and created furniture based on the Larsson philosophy of imperfection, clarity, and simplicity and Kamprad's belief in offering functional, affordable design for all—or, as the company calls it, "democratic design," which IKEA claims is ever-evolving.[13]

IKEA uses the paintings of Carl Larsson and the designs of Karin to help promulgate a certain kind of Swedish sensibility. Those paintings capture Karin Larsson's own unique and iconic style. IKEA's website clarifies this heritage: "In the late 1800s, the artists Carl and Karin Larsson combined classical influences with warmer Swedish folk styles. They created a model of Swedish home furnishing design that today enjoys worldwide renown. In the 1950s the styles of modernism and functionalism were developing at the same time as Sweden was establishing a society founded on social equality. The IKEA product range—modern but not trendy, functional yet attractive, people-focused and child-friendly—carries on these Swedish home furnishing traditions."[14]

Karin's ideas are nowhere more successfully translated than through IKEA. And lately these ideas have also been seen at other stores that stress light and colorful interiors such as Target, Pier One Imports, and West Elm. The courtship and marriage between Karin and IKEA have been very satisfying—almost as meaningful for the consumer and designer as her marriage to Carl Larsson. From the perspective of today, their union seems almost preordained.

In the United States, the ultimate recognition of Karin as a designer, not just a merchandiser for IKEA, came from an exhibition sponsored, in part, again by IKEA at the National Museum of Women in the Arts in Washington, D.C. This exhibition looked at the contributions to style and design made by women from five Nordic countries: Denmark, Finland, Iceland, Norway, and Sweden.

Nordic Cool: Hot Women Designers ran from April 23 until September 12, 2004, and included designers who have changed the course of the decorative arts. The cocurator of the show, Judy L. Larson, said, "This exhibition encourages the understanding of design within the context of culture and gender, presenting works of great beauty in a sociological setting." Karin is noted there among these women as the first designer of what would become known as Swedish Modern.[15]

In Sweden Karin is now seen as a prominent figure in her own right, distinct from her husband. The *Karin Bergöö Larssons vänner* website, as it is called in Swedish, is devoted to Karin, her family, her times, and her lifestyle. She is viewed here without the large shadow of her husband, allowing her to be illuminated in all her glory, as herself, and for herself. The association, Karin Bergöö Larsson's Friends, was formed in 1989 to emphasize Karin and her life's work. This association supports female creation through scholarships. The organization resides in Hallsberg, where Karin spent her childhood, and provides conferences and other events throughout the year at the Bergööhuset, a museum and her family home. One special event each year is in celebration of Karin's birthday, October 3.[16]

Karin Larson was a remarkable woman who transcended her time—and her marriage to a difficult man who did not approve of female artists. She took the "high road." She married a man she loved and raised children—in and of itself, a noble profession. But she also managed to use her talents in a way that did not compromise her relationship or duties as a mother. She made it all work. And as a result, she made the homes and lives of countless people throughout the world a bit more beautiful. Her contributions are recognized by designers and scholars, and her ideas and ideals are seen in every design magazine that one opens: the hardwood floors; the plant-filled rooms; the spare but elegant furnishings; the light coming in from broad, uncovered windows; the neutral colors.

Today the results of Karin's style can be seen all over the world and are most notably recognized in the products of IKEA, one of the most ubiquitous retail home furnishing stores. The yellow-and-blue stores, which are now all over Great Britain and the United States, emphasize a certain type of style used by Karin: "Muslin drapes over the chaise longue, painted floorboards and rag rugs, pickled and limed furniture and cafe curtains halfway across the window, may beautifully capture the current mood of simplicity, but they have their origins in the Gustavian period."[17]

From the school dorm to the most elegant and fashionable of homes, the style used by Karin in her little country estate has been converted into modern Swedish design, which has exerted a significant influence on domestic as well as international interior design.

Chronology

1566–1858	The early years of the Sahlqvist family from Örebro, and the Bergöö family from Sundborn and Falun—Karin's ancestors
1859	On October 3, Karin Bergöö was born in Örebro, Värmland province, Sweden
1862	Karin and her family move to Hallsberg
1873	Karin leaves her family to attend the French School in Stockholm
1875	Karin's father buys a small cottage in Sundborn
1874	Karin transfers to the Arts and Crafts School
1877	Karin is accepted into the Fine Arts Academy in Stockholm
1878	First meeting with Carl Olof Larsson at a ball in Stockholm
1882	Travels throughout Europe to visit important art museums Joins the famous Académie Colarossi art school in Paris Spends summer at Grez-sur-Loing, with Carl Larsson Karin becomes engaged to Carl
1883	Karin and Carl are married in Stockholm on June 12
1884	Daughter Suzanne is born in Grez, France
1887	First son, Ulf, is born
1888	Son Pontus is born in France
1891	Daughter Lisbeth is born
1893	Daughter Brita is born
1894	Son Mats is born, but dies shortly thereafter
1896	Daughter Kersti is born
1897	Karin has a very serious lung inflammation and almost dies

1899	Karin becomes ill again with influenza and is in bed in Stockholm for many months
1900	Son Esbjörn is born
1901	Family moves permanently to Sundborn from Stockholm Karin's mentor and favorite aunt, Elsie Sahlqvist, dies
1905	Son Ulf dies at 18 years of age
1913	Karin's mother Hilda dies
1919	Carl dies on January 22
1924	Karin is 65 years old
1928	Karin dies on February 17
1931	First publication of Carl Larsson's memoir, *Jag* (Myself)
1997	The exhibition at the Victoria and Albert Museum, *Carl and Karin Larsson, Creators of the Swedish Style*

Chapter Notes

Preface

1. Snodin, "Carl and Karin Larsson," 163. According to Lena Rydin.

2. Fortini, "IKEA Forever," M2206. This is the most current data for IKEA.

3. Acknowledgment, taken from IKEA's website titled, "Our Swedish Origins." Available at https://www.ikea.com/ms/en_AU/about_ikea/the_ikea_way/swedish_heritage/index.html.

4. Strindberg, *A New Blue Book*, 612. August Strindberg famously defamed both Carl and Karin in this literary work. His criticism has also been chronicled in a number of works about Carl Larsson and written about by Carl himself in his memoir. Carl devoted a chapter to Strindberg, describing their friendship and their falling out (Larsson, *Jag*, 176–78).

5. Jansson, *Kninnor för sin hatt*, 79–95. A retired history teacher and historian of the city of Hallsberg, Sweden, Jansson wrote about Karin Larsson's aunt, the famous hat maker.

6. The Arts and Crafts School was founded by *Nils Månsson Mandelgren* and in Karin's time was located in Norrmalm, a district in Stockholm between the Church of Saint Clare and *Hötorget* (a square in the center of Stockholm).

7. Tate, *Académie Colarossi*, http://www.tate.org.uk/learn/online-resources/glossary/a/academie-colarossi. The Académie Colarossi was an art school in Paris, France, established in the nineteenth century as an alternative to the official École des Beaux Art.

8. From a conversation with Karin and Carl's granddaughter, at her apartment in Stockholm, where we discussed Karin giving up her art, because, as her granddaughter said, she wanted to.

9. National Museum of Women in the Arts, "Nordic Cool: Hot Women Designers," http://www.scandinaviandesign.com/news/NMWA/.

10. Flanders, *Inside the Victorian Home*, 87. Flanders describes the Victorian home and how it came to be.

11. Key, *Skönhet för alla*, 72. Key, a bold social pioneer, lauded Karin Larsson long before anyone else did. She argued that beauty was not a luxury and that it ennobled and enriched man.

12. The exhibition's slogan was *Acceptera!* (Accept!), which was a literal plea for the acceptance of functionalism, standardization, and mass production as cultural change. The effort to persuade Swedish citizens of the benefits of a modernized lifestyle included serving mass-produced food.

13. H55 was an international exhibition that was considered the first step in heralding Sweden as a leader in design.

14. Eleish and van Breems, *Swedish Interiors*, 137, 163. The authors argue that Karin Larsson ushered in a new appreciation for traditional design.

Chapter 1

1. Snodin, "Looking at Lilla Hyttnäs," 96.

2. Karin Bergöö Larssons vänner website. Blog created by Curt Froberg. See https://translate.google.com/translate?hl=en&sl=sv&u=http://www.karinforeningen.se/antavla/ for more information.

3. *Ibid.*

4. Karin Bergöö Larssons vänner website. See https://translate.google.com/translate?hl=en&sl=sv&u=http://www.karinforeningen.se/adolf-bergoo/ for more information on the merchant Adolf Bergöö—Karin's father.

5. Karin Bergöö Larssons vänner website. See https://translate.google.com/translate?hl=en&sl=sv&u=http://www.karinforeningen.se/hilda-bergoo/ for more information on Hilda Bergöö, born Sahlqvist—Karin's mother.

6. Jansson, "The Bergöö Family" (unpublished document, April 22, 2012), 4.

7. Karin Bergöö Larssons vänner website. See https://translate.google.com/translate?hl= en&sl=sv&u=http://www.karinforeningen.se/ sahlqvist/ for more information on the letter from Hilda Bergöö to Karin Bergöö regarding Karin's birth.

8. Högberg, "The Decline of Maternal Mortality," 1313. The nineteenth century decline in maternal mortality was largely caused by improvement in obstetric care, but was also helped along by the national health strategy of giving midwives and doctors complementary roles in maternity care, as well as equal involvement in setting public health policy.

9. Högberg, Wall, and Broström, "The impact of early medical technology," 252. This information is taken from a historical study of maternal deaths conducted by Högberg in Sweden that analyzed the decline in mortality between 1861 and 1900. During these years maternal mortality was reduced by 76 percent, with female mortality dropping to 33 percent.

10. Frieberg, *Karin*, 24. Karin's son-in-law, Alex Frieberg, wrote about her father.

11. Jansson, "The Bergöö Family" (unpublished document, April 22, 2012), 4.

12. Rydin, *Karin Larsson i närbild*, 14, 15.

13. Jansson, "The Bergöö Family" (unpublished document, April 22, 2012), 5.

14. *Ibid.*

15. The *Riksdag* or Parliament is the national legislature of Sweden and the supreme decision-making body.

16. McKenna, "Sweden: Past and Present," 203.

17. "Railways in Sweden." See https://sinfin. net/railways/world/sweden.html for more information on facts about the Swedish railway system.

18. World History at KMLA, "History of Sweden. Length of railway lines," http://www. zum.de/whkmla/region/scandinavia/xsweden. html#18401864.

19. *Encyclopedia of World Biography*, s.v. "Bremer, Fredrika," http://www.encyclopedia. com/people/literature-and-arts/scandinavian-literature-biographies/fredrika-bremer. In her novel, *Hertha*, Fredrika Bremer dramatized the need for legal rights for women.

20. This popular book by Maria Susanna Cummins was first published in 1854 and is considered a female *bildungsroman*—a type of novel concerned with the education, development, and maturing of a young protagonist. It tells the story of Gertrude Flint, an abandoned, mistreated orphan rescued from an abusive guardian at the age of eight by a lamplighter. Karin's love for this book is documented in Lena Rydin's book about Karin (*Karin Larsson i närbild*, 15).

21. Frieberg, *Karin*, 20.

22. *Ibid.*, 23.

23. SKF has locations all over the world according to their website, http://www.skf.com/us/ our-company/skf-locations-global/index.html.

24. On March 9, 1862, the Civil War battle of Hampton Roads between the ironclads *USS Monitor* and *CSS Virginia* (formerly the *USS Merrimack*) heralded the beginning of a new era in naval warfare. Though indecisive, the battle marked the change from wood and sail to iron and steam, from the *USS Monitor* Center. For more information on the history of this battle, see http://www.monitorcenter.org/the-uss-monitors-story/.

25. Bo E. Ãkermark, a legendary editor for the *Dagens Nyheter*, was quoted by Ulrik Jansson in an unpublished piece about the culture of the Bergöö home in Hallsberg.

26. Frieberg, *Karin*, 21.

27. Rydin, *Karin Larsson i närbild*, 17.

28. Frieberg, *Karin*, 31.

Chapter 2

1. Frieberg, *Karin*, 20.

2. *Ibid.*, 21.

3. *Ibid.*, 22. Karin loved living in Hallsberg.

4. *Ibid.*, 23. Bie is a small spa town in Sweden. Spas and health resorts have been part of Swedish culture for over 300 years. Adolf went frequently to the spa in Bie because of his chronic illnesses.

5. *Ibid.*

6. There is some ambiguity in the literature search as to whether Karin went to the French School first or to the Arts and Crafts School. Most of my translations seem to indicate that Karin went first to the French School, so I choose to follow that path in my storytelling.

7. Karin Bergöö Larssons vänner website, Fröberg. See https://translate.google.com/trans late?hl=en&sl=sv&u=http://karinblogg.karin foreningen.se/ for more information on the train from Hallsberg to Stockholm.

8. Frieberg, *Karin*, 27.

9. *Ibid.*

10. Smorgasbord: The Shortcut to Sweden. See http://www.sverigeturism.se/smorgasbord/ smorgasbord/provincial/stockholm/history/ for more information on the history of Stockholm.

11. Werner, *Nuns and Sisters*, 152.

12. Jansson, "The Bergöö Family" (unpublished document, April 22, 2012), 7–8.

13. *Ibid.*

14. Frieberg, *Karin*, 28.

15. *Ibid.*, 29.

16. Karin Bergöö Larssons vänner website, Fröberg. See https://translate.google.com/translate?hl=en&sl=sv&u=http://karinblogg.karin foreningen.se/ for more information on Karin at 14–15 years of age.

17. *Ibid.*

18. Jansson, "The Bergöö Family" (unpublished document, April 22, 2012), 9.

19. *Ibid.*

20. To blow out an egg, hold up a thin straw to a small hole in the egg then blow air through the straw and into the egg, letting the insides flow out from a larger hole. Keep doing this until the egg is empty.

21. *Swedish Heart and Soul,* "Sweden's Official National Minorities," March 14, 2013, https://andersmoberg676.wordpress.com/2013/03/14/swedens-official-national-minorities/.

22. Jansson, *Karinföredrag vid handarbetets vänners skola* (unpublished document provided to the author by Ulrik Jansson, a Hallsberg historian and author), 5.

23. *Ibid.,* 6.

24. *Ibid.*

25. Griffiths, *Stockholm: A Cultural History,* 9.

26. Jansson, *Karinföredrag vid handarbetets vänners skola* (unpublished document provided to the author by Ulrik Jansson (a Hallsberg historian and author), 8.

27. *Ibid.*

28. "History," Kontsfack University of Arts, Crafts and Design, last updated February 21, 2014, https://translate.google.com/translate?hl=en&sl=sv&u=https://www.konstfack.se/sv/Om-Konstfack/Detta-ar-Konstfack/Historik/&prev=search. The Slöjdskolan (Arts and Crafts School) was founded in 1844 and had an important impact on Swedish arts and crafts. Today it is the University of Arts, Crafts and Design—the Konstfack.

Chapter 3

1. Karin Bergöö Larssons vänner website. See https://translate.google.com/translate?hl=en&sl=sv&u=http://www.karinforeningen.se/&prev=search for more information.

2. *Nature Travels,* "Jultomten: Sweden's Santa Claus," December 4, 2009, https://naturetravels.wordpress.com/2009/12/04/jultomten-swedens-santa-claus/. *Jultomten,* Sweden's Santa Claus, is simply referred to as *Tomten,* or Father Christmas. He visits houses in the afternoon of Christmas Eve, distributing presents to children. He is shown as looking somewhat like the U.S. version of Santa: corpulent figure, red clothes, long white beard. The image is said to be the creation of Jenny Nyström.

3. *Swedish Thoughts.* See http://swedenroots.blogspot.com/2012/06/julia-beck.html for more information on Julia Beck and images of her art.

4. *Google Arts & Culture,* "A Day of Celebration," https://www.google.com/culturalinstitute/beta/asset/a-day-of-celebration/rQGrnUpToLlI-A.

5. Ignell, "Karin Larsson: 10 Years with VÄV," 3, http://en.vävmagasinet.se/wp-content/uploads/2015/06/Karin_Larsson.pdf.

6. Ottilia Adelborg Museum, "Ottilia Adelborg." See https://translate.googleusercontent.com/translate_c?depth=1&hl=en&prev=search&rurl=translate.google.com&sl=sv&u=http://ottiliaadelborgmuseet.se/ottilia-adelborg/&usg=ALkJrhhNh6KTh_pxNJcJrhVLw9pyiAfjaQ for more information.

7. Frieberg, *Karin,* 34.

8. Myers, "Women Artists in Nineteenth-Century France," http://www.metmuseum.org/toah/hd/19wa/hd_19wa.htm.

9. Stanton, *Woman Question in Europe,* 110.

10. *Ibid.,* 205.

11. Larsson, *Carl Larsson,* 87.

12. Barton, *Sweden and Visions of Norway,* 132.

13. Facos, *Nationalism and the Nordic Imagination,* 20.

14. The Palace, "The Sugar Mill That Became a Groundbreaking Art Gallery." See http://www.palace.se/en/opponents for more information on The Opponents.

15. Karin Bergöö Larssons vänner website, https://translate.google.com/translate?hl=en&sl=sv&u=http://www.karinforeningen.se/&prev=search.

16. Wallentinus, Hans-Georg, "Art Schools in Mariefred Neighborhood Years around 1880," https://translate.google.se/translate?hl=en&sl=sv&u=http://www.conec.se/HGW/skrivet/rafsnas/sormlandsbygden.pdf&prev=search.

17. *Ibid.*

18. *Ibid.,* 45

19. Karin Bergöö Larssons vänner website, https://translate.google.com/translate?hl=en&sl=sv&u=http://www.karinforeningen.se/&prev=search.

20. *Ibid.*

Chapter 4

1. Clark, *Women and Achievement,* 95.

2. For more information on the Académie Colarossi, Paris, see http://www.tfsimon.com/academie-colarossi-paris.htm.

3. Nyström painted *Jultomte,* or *Tomte,* legendary creatures from Nordic folklore connected with the Winter Solstice and the Christ-

mas season. Traditionally, they reside in the houses and stables of the farmstead and subtly go about as the family's gatekeepers. They shield the family and animals from harm and mishap, and may likewise help with the tasks and farm work. However, they are known to be grumpy, particularly when affronted.

4. Hanna Pauli came from an artistic family and worked at Académie Colarossi, but later than Karin—although she had studied art in Stockholm from the age of 12 alongside Karin and Eva Bonnier. Hanna's father was editor of musical works and her uncle, Adolf Hirsch, was a painter. Pauli came to Paris in the autumn of 1885 to study at Académie Colarossi under the tutelage of Pascal Dagnan-Bouveret and Raphaël Collin. She eventually married Georg Pauli, whom she met in Barbizon, France. She became a gifted portrait painter, making her debut at the Salon de Paris in 1887, and is arguably the most famous of the female Swedish artists at the time Karin Larsson was painting, in both Sweden and France. Her paintings, *Breakfast Time* (1887) and, her most infamous painting, *The Artist Venny Soldan-Brofelt* (1887), are representative of the art of Swedish women paintings.

5. "Académie Colarossi, Paris," http://www. tfsimon.com/academie-colarossi-paris.htm.

6. Frieberg, *Karin*, 39.

7. Cavalli-Björkman, *Eva Bonnier ett konstnardsliv*, 82.

8. Myers, "The Lure of Montmartre, 1880–1900," http://www.metmuseum.org/toah/hd/mont/hd_mont.htm.

9. From notes provided to me by Karin Larsson's granddaughter and namesake for a presentation she made at Jamestown of Carl and Karin Larsson, Jamestown Community College, 2008.

10. In an article, "Strindberg Ghosts at Hôtel Chevillon," Christian Sundgren wrote about the hotel; for more information on Hôtel Chevillon, see https://translate.google.com/translate?hl=en&sl=sv&u=http://www.nytid.fi/2012/05/strindberg-spokar-pa-hotel-chevillon/&prev=search.

11. Cavalli-Björkman and Lindwall, "The Life and Art of Carl Larsson," 13.

12. Facos, *Nationalism and the Nordic Imagination*, 20.

13. Cavalli-Björkman and Lindwall, "The Life and Art of Carl Larsson," 13.

14. Frieberg, *Karin*, 39.

15. *Ibid.*

Chapter 5

1. Larsson, *Carl Larsson*, 5.
2. *Ibid.*, 6.

3. *Ibid.*, 5.

4. Wikipedia, "History of Stockholm," last modified November 19, 2016, https://en.wikipedia.org/wiki/History_of_Stockholm#cite_note-Andersson-49-56-29.

5. Larsson, *Carl Larsson*, 7.

6. *Ibid.*, 8.

7. Cavalli-Björkman and Lindwall, "Life and Art of Carl Larsson," 9.

8. Larsson, *Carl Larsson*, 10.

9. *Ibid.*, 13.

10. *Ibid.*

11. *Ibid.*, 16.

12. *Ibid.*

13. *Ibid.*, 72.

14. *Ibid.*, 68.

15. *Ibid.*

16. See the Académie Française website, http://www.academie-francaise.fr/, for more information.

17. Cavalli-Bjorkman and Lindwall, "Life and Art of Carl Larsson," 120–125. Here, the theory that Carl Larsson hid his demons behind his family is discussed.

18. *Ibid.*, 10.

19. Larsson, *Carl Larsson*, 81.

20. *Ibid.*, 101.

Chapter 6

1. See *The Victorian Artists*, "Carl Larsson," http://www.avictorian.com/Larsson_Carl.html, for more information.

2. Larsson, *Carl Larsson*, 101.

3. *Ibid.*

4. Larsson, *Carl Larsson*, 101.

5. Frieberg, *Karin*, 44.

6. Larsson, *Carl Larsson*, 102.

7. *Ibid.*

8. Frieberg, *Karin*, 45.

9. Larsson, *Carl Larsson*, 102.

10. *Ibid.*

11. Freiberg, *Karin*, 46.

Chapter 7

1. Cavalli-Björkman and Lindwall, *The World of Carl Larsson*, 13.

2. Rydin, "Karin Larsson," 166.

3. Frieberg, *Karin*, 44.

4. Larsson, *Carl Larsson*, 102.

5. Cavalli-Björkman, "The Life and Art of Carl Larsson," 7.

6. *Ibid.*, 13.

7. *Ibid.*, 12.

8. Larsson, *Carl Larsson*, 81.

9. Gedin, *Karin! Karin! Karin! Min engel!*,

10.

10. *Ibid.*, 9.

11. Rydin, "Karin Larsson," 166.

12. Personal conversation with Carl and Karin's granddaughter, Karin Larsson, who reiterated that she did not feel that her grandmother had any regrets about giving up her life as a painter.

13. Cavalli-Björkman, 89

14. *Ibid.*, 91

15. *Ibid.*, 93

16. *Ibid.*

17. *Swedish Thoughts.* See http://swedenroots.blogspot.com/2012/06/julia-beck.html for more information on Julia Beck.

18. Rydin, *Karin Larsson i närbild*, 20.

19. Larsson, *Carl Larsson*, 104.

20. Description taken from viewing Carl's portrait of Karin, *The Bride.*

21. Cavalli-Björkman, "The Life and Art of Carl Larsson," 22.

22. *Ibid.*

23. Larsson, *Carl Larsson*, 105.

24. Frieberg, *Karin*, 62.

25. Larsson, *Carl Larsson*, 106.

26. Rydin, "Karin Larsson," 166.

27. Larsson, *Carl Larsson*, 111.

28. *Ibid.*

29. Rydin, *Karin Larsson i närbild*, 29.

Chapter 8

1. *Cloude of Océane pages…Carnets de Lecture—Albums of Arts*, "Carl Larsson, A savage and independent Swedish painter," August 11, 2016, https://translate.google.com/translate?hl=en&sl=fr&u=http://aufildespagesavecoceane.hautetfort.com/archive/2016/07/30/carl-larsson-peintre-aquarelliste-suedois-5831918.html&prev=search. Taken from an excerpt written by Georg Nordensvan (1855–1932), a Swedish art historian, critic, and writer. He wrote *Carl Larsson: A Study. Stockholm: Light. 1901.*

2. Information gathered about Spada comes from various places. He has been mentioned as being married to Julia Beck, but I can find only one place that mentions this. I am assuming they were friends and even lovers, but to the best of my knowledge, Julia Beck did not marry. She and Janzon, however, were in the same place many times, especially in Paris. One source about his life can be found on this website, https://translate.googleusercontent.com/translate_c?depth=1&hl=en&prev=search&rurl=translate.google.se&sl=sv&u=https://sok.riksarkivet.se/sbl/Presentation.aspx%3Fid%3D12055&usg=ALkJrhhA-ZGsarqgrywvvBeSFAnpxVT16A/.

3. Spada, *Swedish Pariser Artists*, 2–11, https://translate.google.se/translate?hl=en&sl=sv&u=http://www.karinforeningen.se/wp-content/uploads/2016/04/Jul-i-Grez.pdf&prev=search.

4. Frieberg, *Karin*, 88.

5. Gedin, *Karin! Karin! Karin! Min engel!*, 10.

6. Rydin, "Karin Larsson," 167.

7. Ohlsen, *Lonely Planet Pocket Stockholm*, 79–82.

8. Frieberg, *Karin*, 107–8.

9. Larsson, *Carl Larsson*, 117.

10. Facos, *Nationalism and the Nordic Imagination*, 13.

11. *Ibid.*, 9.

12. *Ibid.*, 13.

13. *Ibid.*

14. *Ibid.*, 180.

15. Frieberg, *Karin*, 110–11.

16. *Ibid.*, 116.

17. Larsson, *Carl Larsson*, 119.

18. *Ibid.*

19. Frieberg, *Karin*, 118.

20. Larsson, *Carl Larsson*, 120.

Chapter 9

1. Frieberg, *Karin*, 122.

2. *Ibid.*, 125.

3. Karin Bergöö Larssons vänner website. See https://translate.google.com/translate?hl=en&sl=sv&u=http://www.karinforeningen.se/ferdinand-boberg/ for more information on Ferdinand Boberg.

4. Karin Bergöö Larssons vänner website. See https://translate.google.com/translate?hl=en&sl=sv&u=http://www.karinforeningen.se/om-bergööska-huset/ for a depiction of the mural that Carl made in the great hall.

5. Snodin, "Looking at Lilla Hyttnäs," 96.

6. Eriksson, "Sweden in the 1890s," 12.

7. Official Visitor Guide: Göteborg, "Haga." See http://www.goteborg.com/en/haga/ for more information on the charming neighborhood of Haga, one of the oldest in Gothenburg, where these little wooden homes have been preserved.

8. Pinterest, "Explore Chair Lillberg, Ikea Rocking Chair, and more!" See https://www.pinterest.com/pin/566820303072348735/ to view images of the IKEA rocking chair designed by Karin Larsson and still sold today, called Lillberg.

9. Blume and *International Herald Tribune*, "Bathing Sweden in Nordic Light," http://www.nytimes.com/1997/12/20/style/bathing-sweden-in-nordic-light.html.

10. Larsson, *Carl Larsson*, 185.

11. *Ibid.*, 128.

12. *Ibid.*
13. Frieberg, *Karin*, 128.
14. *Ibid.*, 132.
15. *Ibid.*, 133.
16. *Ibid.*, 129.
17. *Ibid.*, 133.
18. Lindwall, "Sweden and Paris," 29–30.
19. Frieberg, *Karin*, 130.
20. *Ibid.*, 132.
21. *Ibid.*, 132–133.

Chapter 10

1. Larsson, *Carl Larsson*, 127.
2. Högardh-Ihr, *Karin Larsson och blommorna i Sundborn*, 57, 62, 63.
3. *Ibid.*, 51.
4. Rydin, *Karin Larsson i närbild*, 88.
5. *Ibid.*, 90–91.
6. *William Morris—The Arts and Crafts Movement.* "William Morris," http://www.artyfactory.com/art_appreciation/graphic_designers/william_morris.html. William Morris was a leading member of the Arts and Crafts Movement. He is best known for his pattern designs, particularly on fabrics and wallpapers. His vision in linking art to industry by applying the values of fine art to the production of commercial design was a key stage in the evolution of design as we know it today.
7. Wendy Kaplan, "The Arts and Crafts Movement from England to the United States," lecture, The Charles Hosmer Morse Museum of American Art, Los Angeles, CA, January 14, 2009, http://www.morsemuseum.org/programs-events/lectures/the-arts-and-crafts-movement-from-england-to-the-united-states.
8. Digby, "Victorian Values," 195–215.
9. Abrams, "Ideals of Womanhood in Victorian Britain," 3, http://classwithmpenton.weebly.com/uploads/1/3/6/3/13638874/janeeyreidealsofwomanhoodactivity.pdf.
10. Obniski, "The Arts and Crafts Movement in America," http://www.metmuseum.org/toah/hd/acam/hd_acam.htm.
11. Krippendorff, "Design Pages," 517.
12. Rydin, "Karin Larsson," 169.
13. Key, *Skonhet i hemmen*, 4.
14. Miller, "An Introduction," 19.
15. GlassFromSweden.com, "A Short History of Swedish Glass—How a Nation Conquered the World," http://www.glassfromsweden.com/history-of-swedish-glass.html.
16. Skansen, "About Skansen," http://www.skansen.se/en/artikel/about-skansen-0.
17. Rydin, "Karin Larsson," 169.
18. Krugovoy Silver, "A Caught Dream," 37–44.
19. Stavenow-Hidemark, "A Home of Its Time," 71.
20. *The Free Dictionary*, s.v. *"Japonism,"* accessed January 19, 2017, http://www.thefreedictionary.com/Japonism.
21. Snodin, Introduction to *Carl and Karin Larsson*, 8.
22. Frieberg, *Karin*, 140.
23. *Ibid.*
24. *Ibid.*, 141.
25. *Ibid.*, 143.
26. Lindwall, *Ett hem*, 32.

Chapter 11

1. Frieberg, *Karin*, 143.
2. Carl Larsson, *Motiv från Marstrand* (Motif from Marstrand). See https://www.bukowskis.com/auctions/559/33-carl-larsson-motiv-fran-marstrand to view image of painting.
3. Frieberg, *Karin*, 143.
4. *Ibid.*
5. *Ibid.*, 144.
6. *Ibid.*, 148.
7. *Ibid.*, 149.
8. Lindwall, *Et hem*, 32.
9. Cavalli-Björkman, *Eva Bonnier ett konstnarsliv*, 175.
10. *Ibid.*, 327.
11. Rydin, "Karin Larsson," 166.
12. *Ibid.*, 162.
13. Lindwall, *"Ett hem,"* 32.
14. Rydin, *Karin*, 174, figure 202.
15. *Ibid.*, 171, figure 199.
16. *Ibid.*, 173, figure 200.

Chapter 12

1. Frieberg, *Karin*, 151.
2. Larsson, *Carl Larsson*, 143.
3. Rydin, "Karin Larsson," 167.
4. Frieberg, *Karin*, 154.
5. *Ibid.*, 156.
6. *Ibid.*, 157.
7. *Ibid.*, 156.
8. *Ibid.*
9. Lindwall, *"Ett hem,"* 32.
10. Rydin, "Karin Larsson," 166–167.
11. Topjon, "Ett hem: A2 1899," 2.
12. Rydin, *Carl Larsson-gården*, 42.
13. *Ibid.*, 27, 31–32.
14. Lengefeld, "Translation and Transformation," 196–200.
15. *Ibid.*, 200.
16. Tsaneva, *Carl Larsson: 112 Masterpieces*, 5.
17. Stavennow-Hidemark, "A Home of Its Time," 72.
18. *Ibid.*, 73.

19. Ivanov, *Vackrare vardagsvara*, umu.diva-portal.org/smash/get/diva2:142915/FULL TEXT01.

Chapter 13

1. Frieberg, *Karin*, 167. The translation of this poem into English does not reflect well the poetry of Carl. A rough English translation is:

Now the studio is ready, I have, ha ha.
Airy and just and dignified, just said, just
    said.
When it was here, on the flat, on the flat.
Generally in the parish said, damn, damn.
The shimmer all over the garden, but,
    however,
yet like fully have the star, with the stock
    at the stock.

2. Rydin, *Carl Larsson-gården*, 53.
3. Larsson, *Carl Larsson*, 168.
4. *Ibid.*, 169.
5. Rydin, *Carl Larsson-gården*, 17.
6. Rydin, "Karin Larsson," 172.
7. HV Textil, "Sophie Adlersparre," http://www.hv-textil.se/var-historik/bildarkiv/portratt-av-sophie-adlersparre/.
8. *Idun*, "En Kvinnogärning," February 11, 1901, 68. This article on Karin's Aunt Lisen, the famous hat maker, was published following her death.
9. Frieberg, *Karin*, 169.
10. *Ibid.*, 172.
11. Lengefeld, "Translation and Transformation," 200.
12. Larsson, *Carl Larsson*, 152.
13. Frieberg, *Karin*, 172.
14. Larsson, *Carl Larsson*, 154.
15. Frieberg, *Karin*, 172–173.
16. Larsson, *Carl Larsson*, 152.
17. Frieberg, *Karin*, 174.
18. Rydin, "Karin Larsson," 174.
19. Frieberg, *Karin*, 175.
20. *Ibid.*
21. Köster, "Family Life as a Play," 39.
22. Larsson, *Carl Larsson*, 177–178.
23. *Ibid.*, 152.
24. *Ibid.*, 164.
25. *Ibid.*, 165.
26. Larsson, Karin, "Ett bref från fru Karin," 338.

Chapter 14

1. Larsson, *Carl Larsson*, 190.
2. International Encyclopedia of the First World War, http://encyclopedia.1914-1918-online.net/article/sweden.

3. Rydin, *Karin Larsson i närbild*, 39.
4. Radauer, "Brändström, Elsa," doi:http://dx.doi.org/10.15463/ie1418.10455.
5. Larsson, *Carl Larsson*, 190.
6. *Ibid.*
7. *Ibid.*
8. *Ibid.*
9. Rydin, *Karin Larsson i närbild*, 32.
10. *Ibid.*, 40.
11. The Carl Larsson Trail, www.Carllarsson.se.
12. Köster, "Family Life as a Play," 66–67.
13. Larson, 189.

Chapter 15

1. Larsson, *Carl Larsson*, 164–65.
2. Frieberg, *Karin*, 196.
3. Larsson, *Carl Larsson*, 177.
4. *Ibid.*, 175.
5. *Ibid.*
6. Rydin, *Karin Larsson i närbild*, 168.
7. Frieberg, *Karin*, 202.
8. Larsson, *Carl Larsson*, 189.
9. Rydin, "Karin Larsson," 183.
10. Larsson, *Carl Larsson*, 189.
11. Lindwall, Introduction to *The World of Carl Larsson*, 7.
12. Larsson, *Carl Larsson*, 190.
13. Köster, "Family Life as a Play," 55.
14. Larsson, *Carl Larsson*, 191.
15. Frieberg, *Karin*, 207.
16. *Ibid.*, 208.
17. *Ibid.*
18. *Svenska Dagladet*, Death notice, January 24, 1919.
19. *Göteborgs-Possten*, Obituary, January 23, 1919.
20. Frieberg, *Karin*, 208.
21. *Ibid.*
22. Larsson, Karin, afterward to *Carl Larsson*, 192.
23. Rydin, *Karin Larsson i närbild*, 153.
24. *Ibid.*, 154.
25. Larsson, *Carl Larsson*, ix.

Chapter 16

1. Swedish Design.org, "The Stockholm Exhibition 1930," http://www.swedishdesign.org/Classic/Exibitions/Stockholm-Exhibition/.
2. DN.kultur, The Larsson Furniture Legacy, http://www.dn.se/arkiv/teater/det-larssonska-mobelarvet/.
3. See Snodin and Stavenow-Hidemark, *Carl and Karin Larsson*, 220, for a list of exhibits.
4. Minoli and Costaras, "Preparations for 'Carl and Karin Larsson,'" 4.

5. *Ibid.*

6. *Ibid.*

7. *Ibid.*, 4–5.

8. *The Economist,* "Swedish Design," http://www.economist.com/node/105781.

9. Eleish and van Breems, *Swedish Interiors,* 14.

10. Snodin, *Carl and Karin Larsson: Creators of the Swedish Style,* vi.

11. Swedish Institute, "Ingvar Kamprad," 1, https://sweden.se/business/ingvar-kamprad-founder-of-ikea/.

12. *Ibid.*, 2.

13. IKEA, "Design for Everyone," http://www.ikea.com/ms/en_JP/this-is-ikea/democratic-design/index.html.

14. IKEA, "Our Swedish Origins," http://www.ikea.com/ms/en_KW/about_ikea/the_ikea_way/swedish_heritage/index.html.

15. National Museum of Women in the Arts, "Nordic Cool." See *https://www.utanri kisraduneyti.is/media/Frettatilkynning/Nordic Cool for more information on this* exhibition of women designers.

16. Karin Bergöö Larssons vänner website. See https://translate.google.com/translate?hl=en&sl=sv&u=http://www.karinforeningen.se/ for more information on the Association of Karin Bergöö Larsson's Friends.

17. Niesewand, "Simply Swedish," http://www.independent.co.uk/life-style/simply-swedish-1236628.html.

Bibliography

Abrams, Lynn. "Ideals of Womanhood in Victorian Britain." Unpublished, access date January 15, 2017. http://classwithm penton.weebly.com/uploads/1/3/6/3/ 13638874/janeeyreidealsofwomanhood activity.pdf.

Andersson, Ingrid. *Karin Larsson: Konstnär och konstnärshustru* [Karin Larsson: Artist and artist wife]. Värnamo, Sweden: Gidlunds, 1986.

Barton, H. Arnold. *Sweden and Visions of Norway: Politics and Culture, 1814–1905.* Carbondale, IL: Southern Illinois University Press, 2002.

Blume, Mary, and *International Herald Tribune.* "Bathing Sweden in Nordic Light," *New York Times,* December 20, 1997. http://www.nytimes.com/1997/12/20/ style/bathing-sweden-in-nordic-light. html.

Burkeman, Oliver. "The Miracle of Älmhult." *Guardian,* June 17, 2004. https://www. theguardian.com/lifeandstyle/2004/ jun/17/shopping.retail.

Cavalli-Björkman, Görel. *Carl Larsson: Porträttmålaren* [Carl Larsson: Portrait painter]. Stockholm: Författarförlaget, 1987.

______. *Eva Bonnier: Ett konstnarsliv* [Eva Bonnier: An artistic life]. Stockholm: Albert Bonniers Förlag, 2013.

Cavalli-Björkman, Görel, and Bo Lindwall. "Larsson as Open-Air painter." *The World of Carl Larsson.* Trans. Alan Lake Rice. La Jolla, CA: Green Tiger, 1982. 9–24.

Charles Hosmer Morse Museum of American Art. "The Arts and Crafts Movement from England to the United States." http://www.morsemuseum.org/prog rams-events/lectures/the-arts-and-crafts-movement-from-england-to-the-united-states.

C.L. Garden Sundborn. Carl and Karin Larsson's Family Association. http:// www.carllarsson.se/.

Clark, Linda L. *Women and Achievement in Nineteenth-Century Europe.* New York: Cambridge University Press, 2008.

Clason, Anders. Foreword to *Carl and Karin Larsson: Creators of the Swedish Style.* Ed. Michael Snodin and Elisabet Stavenow-Hidemark. Boston: Bulfinch, 1998. vi.

Digby, Anne. "Victorian Values and Women in Public and Private." *Proceedings of the British Academy* 78 (1992): 195–215.

Economist. "Swedish Design: Where Ikea Got Its Style." November 6, 1997. http:// www.economist.com/node/105781/ print.

Eleish, Rhonda, and Edie van Breems. *Swedish Interiors.* Layton, Utah: Gibbs Smith, 2007.

Eriksson, Eva. "Sweden in the 1890s." *Carl and Karin Larsson: Creators of the Swedish Style.* Ed. Michael Snodin and Elisabet Stavenow-Hidemark. Boston: Bulfinch, 1998. 10–20.

Facos, Michelle. *Nationalism and the Nordic Imagination: Swedish Art of the 1890s.* Berkley: University of California Press, 1998.

Famous Entrepreneurs. "Ingvar Kamprad." http://www.famous-entrepreneurs.com/ ingvar-kamprad.

Flanders, Judith. *Inside the Victorian Home: A Portrait of Domestic Life in Victorian England.* New York: W. W. Norton, 2003.

Fortini, Amanda. "Ikea Forever." *New York*

Times Style Magazine, September 25, 2016.

Frieberg, Axel. *Karin: En bok om Carl Larsson's hustru* [Karin: A book about Carl Larsson's wife]. Stockholm: Albert Bonniers Förlag, 1967.

Frilund, Göran. "The Union's Last War: The Russian-Swedish War of 1808–09." *Military Subjects: Battles & Campaigns.* The Napoleon Series. http://www.napoleon-series.org/military/battles/c_finnish.html.

Gedin, Per I. *Karin! Karin! Karin! Min engel!* [Karin! Karin! Karin! My angel!]. Stockholm: Albert Bonniers Förlag, 2013.

Griffiths, Tony. *Stockholm: A Cultural History.* New York: Oxford University Press, 2009.

Gunnarsson, Torsten. "Carl Larsson: His Life and Art." *Carl and Karin Larsson: Creators of the Swedish Style.* Ed. Michael Snodin and Elisabet Stavenow-Hidemark. Boston: Bulfinch, 1998. 21–52.

Högardh-Ihr, Christina. *Karin Larsson och blommorna i Sundborn* [Karin Larsson and flowers in Sundborn]. Stockholm: Prisma, 2008.

Högberg, Ulf. "The Decline of Maternal Mortality in Sweden: The Role of Community Midwifery." *American Journal of Public Health* 94, no. 8 (August 2004): 1312–20.

Högberg, Ulf, Joseph S. Wall, and Göran Broström. "The Impact of Early Medical Technology on Maternal Mortality in Late 19th Century Sweden." *International Journal of Gynecology & Obstetrics* 24, no. 4 (August 1986): 251–61.

Ignell, Tina. "Karin Larsson. 10 Years with VÄV." *Vävmagasinet* (February 2004). http://en.vävmagasinet.se/wp-content/uploads/2015/06/Karin_Larsson.pdf.

IKEA. "Design for Everyone." https://www.ikea.com/ms/en_KR/Local_homepage/Design_For_Everyone.html.

IKEA. "Hej! Welcome to a world of inspiration for your home." http://www.ikea.com/.

IKEA. "Our Swedish Origins: Historical Influences." https://www.ikea.com/ms/en_AU/about_ikea/the_ikea_way/swedish_heritage/index.html.

Ivanov, Gunnela. *Vackrare vardagsvara—design för alla?: Gregor Paulsson och Svenska Slöjdföreningen 1915–1925* [More beautiful things for everyday use: Gregor Paulsson and the Swedish Society 1915–1925]. January 2004. umu.diva-portal.org/smash/get/diva2:142915/FULLTEXT01.

Jansson, Ulrik. *Kvinnor för sin hatt i 1800-talets Hallsberg.* [Women and their hats in 1900 Hallsberg] HÅFTAD, Svenska, 2013.

Key, Ellen. *Skönhet för alla* [Beauty for everyone]. Uppsala, 1899.

______. "Skönhet i hemmen" [Beauty in the home]. *Idun* 50 (1897): 4.

Köster, Hans-Curt. "Family Life as a Play." *The World of Carl Larsson.* Trans. Alan Lake Rice. La Jolla, CA: Green Tiger, 1982. 44–70.

Krippendorff, Klaus. "Design." *International Encyclopedia of Communication Theory and Philosophy.* Ed. K. Bruhn Jensen and R. T. Craig. Hoboken, NJ: Wiley-Blackwell, 2016. 515–527.

______. *The Semantic Turn: A New Foundation for Design.* New York: CRC Press, 2005.

Krugovoy Silver, Anna. "A Caught Dream: John Ruskin, Kate Greenaway, and the Erotic Innocent Girl." *Children's Literature Association Quarterly* 25, no. 1 (2000): 37–44.

Larsson, Carl. *Andras barn* [Other people's children]. Stockholm: Albert Bonniers Förlag, 1910.

______. *Åt solsidan* [On the sunny side]. Stockholm: Albert Bonniers Förlag, 1910.

______. *Carl Larsson: The Autobiography of Sweden's Most Beloved Artist.* Ed. John Z. Lofgren. Trans. Anne B. Weissmann. Iowa City: Penfield, 1992.

______. *De mina.* [My loved ones]. Stockholm: Albert Bonniers Förlag, 1895.

______. *Ett hem* [A home]. Stockholm: Albert Bonniers Förlag, 1899.

______. *The Larssons.* Stockholm: Albert Bonniers Förlag, 1902.

______. *Spadarfvet—mitt lilla lantbruk* [A farm]. Stockholm: Albert Bonniers Förlag, 1906.

Larsson, Karin. "Ett bref från fru Karin" [A letter from wife Karin]. *Idun,* May 25, 1913.

Larsson, Lena. "The Larsson Design Legacy:

A Personal View." *Carl and Karin Larsson: Creators of the Swedish Style.* Ed. Michael Snodin and Elisabet Stavenow-Hidemark. Boston: Bulfinch, 1998. 220.

Lengefeld, Cecilia. "Translation and Transformation: Carl Larsson's Books in Europe." *Carl and Karin Larsson: Creators of the Swedish Style.* Ed. Michael Snodin and Elisabet Stavenow-Hidemark. Boston: Bulfinch, 1998. 196–211.

Lindgren, Bo Gunnar. Svenska slöjdföreningen. Svenska S H55, Hälsingborg Exhibition 1955: international exhibition of architecture, industrial design, home furnishings and crafts: arranged by the City of Hälsingborg and the Swedish Society of Industrial Design, 10 June–28 August: guide. Jillbergs Bokhandel; 1955.

Lindqvist, Ursula. "The Cultural Archive of the Ikea Store." *Space and Culture* 12 (2009): 43–62, 44.

Lindwall, Bo. "Ett hem" [A home]. *The World of Carl Larsson.* Trans. Alan Lake Rice. La Jolla, CA: Green Tiger, 1982. 30–32.

_____. Introduction to *The World of Carl Larsson.* Trans. Alan Lake Rice. La Jolla, CA: Green Tiger, 1982. 5–12.

_____. "Sweden and Paris, 1885–1889." *The World of Carl Larsson.* Trans. Alan Lake Rice. La Jolla, CA: Green Tiger, 1982. 25–430.

Lübbren, Nina. *Rural Artists' Colonies in Europe, 1870–1910: Places of Nostalgia.* New Brunswick, NJ: Rutgers University Press, 2001.

Manoli, Tina, and Nicola Costaras. "Preparations for 'Carl and Karin Larsson: Creators of the Swedish Style.'" *Conservation Journal,* no. 25 (October 1997). http://www.vam.ac.uk/content/jour nals/conservation-journal/issue-25/pre parations-for-carl-and-karin-larsson-creators-of-the-swedish-style/.

McKenna, Amy. "Sweden: Past and Present." *The Britannica Guide to Countries of the European Union: Denmark, Finland, and Sweden.* Ed. Amy McKenna. New York: Rosen Education Service, 2013. 174–218.

Midvinterblot, Stockholm 1983. Utg. Historiska museet. (Historia i fickformat.) [The historical museum pocket history] Nordensvan, Georg: Carl Larsson I–II, Stockholm 1920–21. (Sveriges allmänna konstförenings publikation.)

Miller Lane, Barbara. "An Introduction to Ellen Key's 'Beauty in the Home.'" *Modern Swedish Design: Three Founding Texts.* Ed. Lucy Creagh, Helena Kåberg, and Barbara Miller Lane. New York: Museum of Modern Art, 2008. 19–31.

Myers, Nicole. "The Lure of Montmartre, 1880–1900." *Heilbrunn Timeline of Art History.* New York: Metropolitan Museum of Art, 2007. http://www.metmuse um.org/toah/hd/mont/hd_mont.htm.

_____. "Women Artists in Nineteenth-Century France." *Heilbrunn Timeline of Art History.* New York: Metropolitan Museum of Art, 2008. http://www.met museum.org/toah/hd/19wa/hd_19wa. htm.

National Museum of Women in the Arts. "Women's Contributions to the Unparalleled Style and Innovation that Define Design from the Five Nordic Countries in Nordic Cool: Hot Women Designers, April 23–Sept. 12, 2004." Press release, March 18, 2004. http://www.scandina viandesign.com/news/NMWA/.

Niesewand, Nonie. "Simply Swedish." *The Independent.* October 17, 1997. http:// www.independent.co.uk/life-style/ simply-swedish-1236628.html.

Nordensvan, Georg. *Carl Larsson: En studie* [Carl Larsson: A study]. Stockholm: Albert Bonniers Förlag, 1901.

_____. *Carl Larsson: En studie.* Stockholm 1906 och 1908. (Småskrifter. Studentföreningen Verdandi).

Obniski, Monica. "The Arts and Crafts Movement in America." *Heilbrunn Timeline of Art History.* New York: Metropolitan Museum of Art, 2008. http://www. metmuseum.org/toah/hd/acam/hd_ acam.htm.

Ohlsen, Becky. *Lonely Planet Pocket Stockholm.* 2nd ed. Melbourne: Lonely Planet Publications, 2004.

Puvogel, Renate. *Carl Larsson: Watercolours and Drawings,* Köln: Benedikt Taschen, 1994.

Qvarnström, Sofi. "Sweden." *1914–1918 Online, International Encyclopedia of the First World War.* Freie Universität Berlin, 2014. Last modified August 14, 2015. http://dx.doi.org/10.15463/ie1418.10150.

Radauer, Lena. "Brändström, Elsa." *1914–1918 Online, International Encyclopedia of the First World War.* Freie Universität Berlin, 2014. Last modified November 1, 2016. http://dx.doi.org/10.15463/ie1418.10455.

Rydberg, Sven. *Stora Kopparberg: 1000 Years of an Industrial Activity.* Stockholm: Gullers International AB, 1979.

Rydin, Lena. *Carl Larsson-gården: Ett hem (a home, ein heim).* Malung: Dalaförlaget, 1994.

_____. "Karin Larsson." *Carl and Karin Larsson: Creators of the Swedish Style.* Ed. Michael Snodin and Elisabet Stavenow-Hidemark. Boston: Bulfinch, 1998. 100–183.

_____. *Karin Larsson i närbild: Allkonstnär och målarhustru från A till Ö.* Stockholm: Forum, 1998.

Sittig, Linda Harris. "Strong Women in History." https://strongwomeninhistory.wordpress.com/2014/01/02/karin-bergoo-by-linda-harris-sittig/.

Sjöberg, Lars, and Ursula Sjöberg. *The Swedish Room.* London: Francis Lincoln, 1994.

Snodin, Michael. "Looking at Lilla Hyttnäs." *Carl and Karin Larsson: Creators of the Swedish Style.* Ed. Michael Snodin and Elisabet Stavenow-Hidemark. Boston: Bulfinch, 1998. 88–159.

_____. Introduction to *Carl and Karin Larsson: Creators of the Swedish Style.* Ed. Michael Snodin and Elisabet Stavenow-Hidemark. Boston: Bulfinch, 1998. 1–9.

Spada. *Swedish Pariser Artists in Hvardagslag.* Stockholm: P. A. Norstedt, 1913.

Stanton, Theodore. *The Woman Question in Europe: A Series of Original Essays.* Boston: Cambridge University Press, 2015.

Stavenow-Hidemark, Elisabet. "A Home of Its Time—But Completely Different." *Carl and Karin Larsson: Creators of the Swedish Style.* Ed. Michael Snodin and Elisabet Stavenow-Hidemark. Boston: Bulfinch, 1998. 53–72.

Strindberg, August. *Carl Larsson: Ett svenskt porträtt med fransk bakgrund* [Carl Larsson: A Swedish portrait with French background]. Göteborg: Rundqvist, 1971.

_____. "En ny blå bok" [A new blue book]. *The Cambridge Companion to August Strindberg.* Ed. Michael Robinson. Boston: Cambridge University Press, 2009.

Swedish Institute. "Ingvar Kamprad, Founder of Ikea." Last updated January 29, 2018. https://sweden.se/business/ingvar-kamprad-founder-of-ikea/.

Thorell, Margaret. "Carl and Karin Larsson: The Muses behind Ikea." *Schuylkill Valley Journal* (June 2016): 147–158. http://www.svjlit.com/features/ikea-and-its-muses-by-magaret-thorell/.

_____. "Karin Bergöö Larsson: Mother, Muse, and Artist." *The Local.* December 9, 2008. http://www.thelocal.se/20081209/16236.

_____. *Swedes of the Delaware Valley.* Charleston: Arcadia, 2011.

Topjon, Ann J. *Carl Larsson: An Annotated Bibliography.* New Castle, DE: Oak Knoll, 2009.

Tsaneva, Maria. *Carl Larsson: 112 Masterpieces.* Seattle: CreateSpace Independent Publishing Platform, 2015.

Vessby, Johan, and Johansson Hadar. *Hos Carl Larsson i Sundborn* [Carl Larsson in Sundborn]. Uppsala, 1930.

Von Zweigbergk, Eva. *Hemma hos Carl Larsson* [The home of Carl Larsson]. Stockholm: Albert Bonners Förlag, 1969.

Werner, Yvonne Maria. *Nuns and Sisters in the Nordic Countries after the Reformation: Female Counter-Culture in Modern Society.* Uppsala: Swedish Institute of Mission Research, 2004.

Index

Numbers in **bold italics** indicate pages with illustrations

www.ingramcontent.com/pod-product-compliance
Ingram Content Group UK Ltd.
Pitfield, Milton Keynes, MK11 3LW, UK
UKHW041355190726
13851UKWH00014B/124